THE COMMONWEALTH AND

Joint Chairmen of the Honorary Editoria

SIR ROBERT ROBINSON, O.M., F.R.S., LO

DEAN ATHELSTAN SPILHAUS, MINNESOT

C000090891

Sept . 1973

SOCIAL STUDIES

General Editor: A. H. RICHMOND

Methods of Social Research

Methods of
Social Research

BY

MARGARET STACEY

PERGAMON PRESS
OXFORD · NEW YORK · TORONTO
SYDNEY · BRAUNSCHWEIG

PERGAMON PRESS LTD.,
Headington Hill Hall, Oxford

PERGAMON PRESS INC.,
Maxwell House, Fairview Park, Elmsford, New York 10523

PERGAMON OF CANADA LTD.,
207 Queen's Quay West, Toronto 1

PERGAMON PRESS (AUST.) PTY. LTD.,
19a Boundary Street, Rushcutters Bay, N.S.W. 2011, Australia

VIEWEG & SOHN GMBH,
Burgplatz 1, Braunschweig

First edition 1969

Reprinted 1970

Library of Congress Catalog Card No. 69–12810

Printed in Great Britain by A. Wheaton & Co., Exeter

08 013354 1 (flexicover)
08 013355 X (hard cover)

Contents

List of Figures

List of Tables

Preface

THE object of this book is to provide an introduction to some of the methods of social research for students who are approaching the subject for the first time. These may be students of sociology at university or technical college, or administrators who find themselves called upon to make or cooperate in some social investigation. The book has been written with Commonwealth as well as British students in mind.

There is some popular tendency to confuse social research with the sample social survey. This book has therefore sought to show that sample surveys are only one method among many of undertaking social research.

It has been impossible to cover every technique and every method, or to illustrate from every area of study. Some subjects, such as socio-historical research, attitude testing, and sociometry, have been ignored altogether. The aim, indeed, was not to be inclusive, but rather to indicate the breadth of the subject, selecting particularly those types of research where, through my own fieldwork or through supervision of graduate students, I have a special interest and knowledge.

This, like every other sociological work I have undertaken, owes a very great deal to the early training given me in the theories and methods of sociology by Professor M. Ginsberg at the London School of Economics during the Second World War. I would also like to acknowledge the daily help of colleagues, both staff and students, who have helped me to see and to try to solve problems. In particular I would like to thank Colin Bell for reading and criticizing the typescript, Richard Startup for certain specific statistical advice, June Pratten for typing the manuscript and Sandra Johns the indices. I would also like to acknowledge gratefully Professor A. Richmond's criticism of the original text and his suggested improvements. Needless to say, no one but myself is answerable for the facts reported and the views expressed here.

Finally, my thanks go to Frank, my husband, and the children, Pat, Richard, Kate, Peter, and Michael, for helping me to combine the role of wife-mother with the gainful occupation of university lecturer.

MARGARET STACEY

School of Social Studies
  University College
  Swansea
  July 1967

CHAPTER 1

The Scientific Method

THERE are many techniques of social investigation, but those that will be dealt with in this book have an important feature in common: they all use the scientific method and are undertaken in a spirit of free inquiry. This attitude underlying research into social matters is at least as important as the detail of the methods used. A particular technique can be turned to any end: it is a tool which can be used or misused, either deliberately or from ignorance.

The types of social investigation with which this book will be concerned are those which honestly set out to increase our knowledge of the facts of social life or to further our understanding of social relations. It is concerned with studies which aim to "prove a theory" only so long as the investigator sets out in the spirit of one who says "I have an idea, let's see if it is true" and is entirely willing to have his hypotheses disproved. Indeed, more than this: he must try as hard as he can to disprove the theory, to see if it will stand up to destructive tests. Only when he has done this is he in a position to say: "I think this theory is right, and so far neither I nor anybody else has been able to disprove it."

The scientific method implies that there is no limit to human knowledge, that it is most unlikely that anyone ever has the final answer, that there is always more to learn, that it is hard to imagine the day when the frontiers of knowledge have been pushed right back. Indeed, it assumes that that place is at infinity and cannot be reached. Nevertheless, the frontiers can be pushed back, the exercise is worth doing, knowledge can be increased, and sometimes a really exciting breakthrough is made.

Humility, then, is an important presupposition for satisfactory social research; humility in the face of the contributions of others and of the immensity of the subject. It is necessary for the researcher to relate his work to that of others and build on what they have done. This is why there are rules and conventions about making proper acknowledgements to other workers and adequate references to their work (although one sometimes suspects the convention is misused to display erudition). In this way all the pieces of new knowledge may be fitted together and one description checked against another, or one interpretation tested against another. It is also why it is most important that data should be collected in ways comparable with other data.* Since the researcher must be willing to be proved wrong he should always try and set out the evidence for his conclusions or for the statements that he is making fully and fairly. This means that he should set the evidence out in such a way that someone else could possibly draw a different conclusion from them, or use the evidence in a different way, or, if the conclusion is apparently inescapable, that the reader should be able to work his own way through the evidence to it.

This is much easier said than done. Distortion can creep in at many points. Even if there is no deliberate intention to mislead, or to twist the evidence, it is easy to do so quite unconsciously. Human bias may enter any scientific work and social research is particularly susceptible to this source of error. Since we are all human we are all involved in what we are studying when we try to study any aspect of social relations. It is part of us. This is true whether we are studying social situations familiar or unfamiliar to us. We may be shocked by behaviour which is different from that which we are used to and have learned to think is right, or we may be so overwhelmed by the differences that our observations are not sufficiently discriminating. When looking at situations we already know, we may fail to see important social features because they are part of a landscape whose familiarity makes us uncritical even if it makes us contemptuous. Our own interests and our own biases may not only enter in the course of doing the research, but will

*Of this more will be said later. See pp. 9–10, 139–40.

have already entered in our choice of research. We chose it either because we have a special interest in it, or because we want to avoid some other aspect which we cannot face for some reason, or because this is research which persons with power and authority wish done and are willing to pay for. We all have a set of expectations about what is the proper way to behave in social relations, and judgements about the value we accord to ideas and to individuals. We cannot get rid of our preferences, our prejudices, or of our value judgements. Nor do I believe that it is possible to draw a hard and fast line between X the research worker and X the citizen with the rights and duties that go with citizenship. Adopting a neutral political or social role is no answer to this problem, for neutrality is a position with attached attitudes. What we can and should do is to understand ourselves and our social positions, to be aware of what our own interests and biases are, and, in so far as this is possible, why we have them. Having made our positions and biases clear to ourselves there is a case for making them overt to others, but if we have been honest with ourselves this is far less difficult. As Polonius said to Laertes: "To thine own self be true, . . . thou canst not then be false to any man" (*Hamlet*). Nevertheless, there are certain conventions which can be followed which will assist us in applying these principles to any actual piece of research. For example, it is probably wise not to be involved in public controversy about a matter which is a current subject of research. The danger of such controversy is twofold. One, that it may lead others to distrust the rigour of the tests which one is applying to the matter in hand. Two, and even more important, it may lead to emotional involvement of a kind that tends to reduce clear thinking by the research worker. It is much harder to be prepared to have a theory disproved if one has committed oneself to it publicly. On the other hand, there may be situations in which such public involvement is felt to be inescapable because of the importance of the values involved. Where, in practice, the line should be drawn between involvement and non-involvement must, of course, be decided for himself by each research worker. The important point is that he should be aware that he has a position, even if it is one of hesitation or attempted neutrality, for these are not value-free positions.

It is useful for social research to be done by more than one person in collaboration, quite apart from the technical reasons, such as the scale and complication of the work and the number of skills needed. Team work can help to reduce individual biases. Thus in the first Banbury Survey[1] the final team was made up of mixed sexes, of one person from the upper class, liable to inherit a title at any time, one lower middle class ex-suburbanite, and one person who had come from a working-class family. In terms, therefore, of the social attitudes which we had acquired as a result of our sex roles and of the social position ascribed to us by our families of origin, we were able to compensate for each other's biases. A similar technique was used by Davis and Gardner in *Deep South* where a Negro couple and a white couple worked together.[2] These collaborations can compensate for some biases, but if the team is working well together it is likely they have some views in common. At a minimum, perhaps, members share the view that the kind of work they are doing is worth while, or that these are the right methods to use. Thus a team may have a tendency to reinforce some individual biases as well as compensating for others.

There is another, cruder but sometimes more difficult, problem that may arise. This is when a commercial firm or a government may ask a worker to undertake research to show that a particular view or action of the firm or government is right. Such a study can only be called scientific if the firm or government accepts that the results may prove them wrong.

Sometimes a similar problem appears at the report stage of a study undertaken in good faith, when it appears that part or all of the findings will offend a particular section of the population. "This", as Nels Anderson has said, "is a problem continually faced by social scientists under dictator governments."[3] Here is a sharp case of what continually occurs, particularly in applied research, of making the best compromise possible between academic integrity and the exigencies of the situation. Again, the important thing is that the scientist should be quite clear what he is doing. He should understand that the withholding of certain results, or the presenting of them in such a way that only fellow workers will see and understand, is a compromise between two sets of values—an uneasy choice. Such choices constantly face us since, as Ginsberg has said, "We have to assume a plurality of values."[4] It may be inevitable that bias will enter the research method or that, given the circumstance, some findings must be suppressed or concealed. In both cases the result will at best retard the development of knowledge about the subject and may well lead to confused thinking and work along blind alleys. A thesis which organizes data to "make a good case" for somebody's cherished beliefs will be demolished in the long run, but it may waste a lot of time meanwhile.

Which of the pressures bears most heavily upon those doing research will depend a good deal on the kind of research that is being undertaken. The reasons for doing the research fall generally speaking into two groups "pure" and "applied". In the first case the principal object is simply to add to the sum total of human knowledge; in the second case, to find out how to do something about a particular practical problem. As Selltiz et al. have said, these two reasons "are at times discussed as if they were somehow opposed or mutually exclusive, and frequently as if one were better than the other. Such an approach is misleading".[5] It is clear that sometimes useful ideas emerge out of "pure" research, and that findings of great importance for theoretical development can arise in the course of applied research. The Banbury study was undertaken as a piece of fundamental research, just to try and see what happened when a modern factory and large numbers of immigrants were brought into an old country town. The focus was on the consequences for the social structure and culture of the town. Subsequently, there has been an increased interest in "overspill" populations, in the development of new towns, and the expansion of old towns. Consequently the Banbury research is sometimes referred to by planners involved in the problems of town expansion, although it was not designed as a piece of applied research. Durkheim's Suicide was a study of a particular social problem which has had far-reaching theoretical and methodological results.[6]

Indeed, Durkheim intended that it should. When research is done within a university it tends to be for academic reasons to further the body of knowledge (although it must be admitted that motives are rarely pure and many a Ph.D is done with the more urgent object of getting a better job than of serving science). Universities may and do undertake applied research also, either on their own initiative, because a member has spotted a problem that needs solving, or because they are asked to by an outside agency. Government departments may undertake their own research or may employ an agency or a university to do it for them. Agencies doing research may be profit-making, taking commissions from anybody for work they want done, or they may be non-profit making existing for a particular purpose.

The pressures that the research workers will feel, and the consequent biases in their work, are likely to be different according to the authority under which they work and its financial source. Pressures of some kind will always be present. The conditions of scientific work will only be fulfilled where the research worker shows an active concern for the scientific method.

HYPOTHESIS OR EXPLORATION

Some people consider that a piece of social research is not scientific unless it has a clearly defined hypothesis which it sets out to test. This would appear to be too narrow a view. In an unknown field it is not possible to set up sufficiently clear hypotheses for testing to form a basis for research.

Hypotheses which are worth testing can only be developed in areas about which a good deal is known, i.e. where a great deal of empirical field data has already been collected. Before this stage most research is of an exploratory nature. The concepts are highly abstract and the possible connections between relevant conditions in real life consequently vague. It is only after much empirical data has been collected and a series of simple relationships, close to reality, have been established, that either precise hypotheses can be enunciated for testing or theory derived inductively from empirical data.

Two cases may serve to illustrate this point. Giddens[7] has shown how, before Durkheim came to tackle the problem of suicide, there had been nearly a century's study of the problem. A number of empirical generalizations had been established connecting suicide rates with urban and rural areas, with different peoples, with different times of the year or day. Durkheim took all these studies, scrutinized them, added some original work of his own (with Marcel Mauss) and from the result developed a method of study and built a theory of suicide which has stood the test of time. Without the patient work of his predecessors all over Europe he would have been unable to achieve this.

The second example is of a quite different and more recent kind. In 1956 Bossard and Boll[8] undertook a study of the large family system. This had a clear conceptual framework, a theory that the size of the family was likely to affect social relations within it. This theory was based upon an application to the family of earlier theory about the effects of the numbers of people in a group upon the social relations of the group. In applying the theory to the family, Bossard and Boll were making it one degree more specific and to this extent less abstract. At the same time, so little was known about the effects upon social relations of the size of the family, that Bossard and Boll could not formulate precise hypotheses, but rather had to explore. They therefore studied some 100 large families in considerable detail, using written life histories and interviewing. Their work was not systematic in the sense that the 100 large families were not a mirror image of all large families, or in that they got precisely the same data from each. This did not matter because Bossard and Boll did not intend that it should be so. They merely wished to collect enough data to show whether it looked likely that the size of the family affected social relations within it, and if so, in what ways did these effects appear. That is to say they wanted to collect data on the basis of which their generalization about size and relationship could be made more precise in its application to family size. Their work was fruitful in the way they intended. Some years later Elder[9] took a number of detailed hypotheses from their exploratory work which he tested with considerable rigour upon particular selected groups. Elder's results are not, of themselves, adequate to build a scientific theory of how social relationships within the family vary with its size. Many more specific studies making particular generalizations will be needed before the tentative theory put forward by Bossard and Boll, as a result of their exploratory work, can be developed into a logical set of propositions which will stand the test of time, i.e. of repeated attempts to refine or disprove it.

Goode and Hatt[10] take the view that it is essential to have an hypothesis to guide research, i.e. a statement of the object of research which may be deduced from existing theory and which will lead to an empirical test. For them an area of study is not an hypothesis. They admit that research workers may at times be justified in exploring an area without a precise hypothesis. Before doing so they should ask why, and, Goode and Hatt predict, their answer is likely to be either a value judgement or an hypothesis. Selltiz et al.[11] accept the value of research into an area in order to reach an hypothesis. Their view is much nearer that of the present author. Whether or not one accepts a highly abstract and generalized statement of a probable relationship as an hypothesis when applied to a given field may be a question of degree. If Goode and Hatt would agree that Bossard and Boll were stating an hypothesis when they said that there were likely to be differences in the social relations within families of different sizes then there is no disagreement here. The statement is not, however, a specific proposition about these relationships, and Bossard and Boll's research was an exploration into the area of the large family to discover such specific propositions or hypotheses. Furthermore, an exploration into an area is bound to be based upon some assumptions, i.e. upon some theory, and it is well to make these explicit, however abstract and distant from the phenomenon in question they may be. As John Madge says,[12] "... virtually all empirical enquiry is based on some theoretical grounds, however naïve these may be". Furthermore, any general body of theory can only be built out of many small generalizations.

THE VALUE OF REPLICATION AND COMPARABILITY

It is, therefore, most important not only that many pieces of empirical work should be going on continuously in many places, but that they should be undertaken in such a way that they will fit together like the pieces of a jigsaw. This means that research should be comparable as far as possible over space and time. It is also important that a piece of work undertaken by one research worker or team should be replicated by other research workers or teams. Only in this way can one become sure that the relationships established are general and not idiosyncratic or unique.

To deal with comparability first: we are all aware of the difficulties of translating English miles into kilometres and of learning to measure temperature in degrees Centigrade when we were brought up to use the Fahrenheit scale. We are aware of the problems of pricing goods when moving from one nation to another when not only are the currencies of each country different, but their values against each other shift from day to day.

These examples, and particularly the last, describe the kind of difficulty that can arise when research workers do not take pains to make their research comparable with that of other workers in the field. It may well be that one finds unsatisfactory definitions or classifications that have been used previously and therefore invents new and improved ones. This is reasonable and necessary for the progress of science. There is, nevertheless, an obligation on any research worker who proposes to do this to use, as well as his own definition or classification, the previously used ones, and to provide a conversion table. In this way his work may be related to and compared with the work which used the previous type of classification. This can also be important when comparison with national data collected by government authority is involved. This will be discussed more fully in a later chapter, which deals with official sources.

Goode and Hatt take the view that the replication of previous studies "does not go beyond checking findings and it is likely to make no contribution to new knowledge".[13] The assumption here, that an hypothesis which has once been tested and shown to relate to the empirical data can then be regarded as true and pass directly to theory seems to contradict the scientific theory of proof which Goode and Hatt have themselves so well expounded in their earlier chapters. The same hypothesis must be checked time and time again before it can be said that the relationship it states has been proved. As Bendix has said, if it has been shown that X goes with Y, it is also necessary to see if X goes with non-Y.[14] This can only be done by testing over and over again the relationship between X and Y. As Selltiz *et al.* point out it is important that, whatever subject is observed, the problem must be formulated in such a way that other observations can be made in the same way. This makes replication possible which, as they say, "is essential to the development of confidence in research findings".[15] As Goode and Hatt themselves say, "Reputations are frequently made by young men through finding holes in the work of older scientists" and that "the scientist must always be willing to throw aside his ideas in the face of contrary evidence".[16] It is, indeed, essential to the scientific spirit that he should look for the contrary evidence and that he should so set up his work that others can do the same.

REFERENCES

1. STACEY, M., *Tradition and Change: A Study of Banbury*, O.U.P., 1960.
2. DAVIS, A., GARDNER, B., and GARDNER, M. R., *Deep South: A Social Anthropological Study of Caste and Class*, 1941.
3. ANDERSON, N., *Our Industrial Urban Civilization*, Asia Publishing House, London, 1964, p. 108.
4. GINSBERG, M., *On Justice in Society*, Heinemann, 1965, p. 44.
5. SELLTIZ, C., JAHODA, M., DEUTSCH, M., and COOK, S. W., *Research Methods in Social Relations*, revised one-volume edition, Henry Holt, 1959, p. 4.
6. DURKHEIM, E., *Suicide*, trans. J. A. Spaulding and G. Simpson (Ed. G. Simpson), Free Press, New York, 1951.
7. GIDDENS, A., The suicide problem in French sociology, *Brit. J. Sociol.* **16**, 3 (1965).
8. BOSSARD, J. H. S., and BOLL, E. S., *The Large Family System*, University of Pa. Press, 1956.

9. ELDER, G. H., Structural variations in the child-rearing relationship, *Sociometry*, **25,** 252 (1962).

   ELDER, G. H. JR., and BOWERMAN, C. E., Family structure and child-rearing patterns: the effect of family size and sex composition, *Am. Sociol. Rev.* **28,** 891 (1963).

10. GOODE, W. J., and HATT, P. K., *Methods in Social Research*, McGraw-Hill, 1952, pp. 57 *et seq.*

11. SELLTIZ *et al., op. cit.*, p. 35 *et seq.*

12. MADGE, J., *The Tools of Social Science*, Longmans, 1965, p. 9.

13. GOODE and HATT, *op. cit.*, p. 58.

14. BENDIX, R., Concepts and generalizations in comparative social studies, *Am. Sociol. Rev.* **28,** 536 (1963).

15. SELLTIZ *et al., op. cit.*, p. 46.

16. GOODE and HATT, *op. cit.*, p. 21.

CHAPTER 2

Fields of Investigation

As THE previous chapter showed there are two main reasons for doing research: one is to try and solve a practical problem and the other is to find out how something works just because it is interesting to know. There are, of course, an almost infinite number of social problems of practical and/or intellectual interest that it would be rewarding to investigate. Depending on their time, place, and personal interests, sociologists have isolated different problems. For purposes of illustration five different types of research will be taken here, differing either in the motivation for the research which leads to a particular problem being studied, or in the ways in which the area for study is defined. The five types are not mutually exclusive.

The first is the investigation of a particular social problem. In this case research is done because some person or authority feels that something is wrong and ought to be put right, or that something could be done better than it is being done at the moment. In this case the problem almost always defines the area of study. The second are studies which are made of a particular social institution or process, such as the family, monogamy, or stratification which is undertaken because people are interested to see how this particular institution or process works in a specific context or in a number of different social contexts. The third is where a particular locality, the people living in a particular place or belonging to a particular social system, are defined as the subject of study. In this case the interest is in seeing how the different aspects of their life, its social structure and culture, are composed, and how the component parts are related to each other to form a coherent whole, or part of a larger whole or wholes. The fourth is a combination of two and three, i.e. the study of a particular institution or process in one locality. The final type of research is one which is undertaken to test a particular theory. This may be a widely held popular or political theory, such as researches which have examined carefully and rejected views about racial inequality once held by some academics and many politicians. Such pieces of research are often closely linked with the first type and have a connection with a particular social problem. Alternatively, and some would say more properly, detailed studies may be made to test a particular hypothesis within a theory, such as Elder's studies mentioned in the previous chapter.★

These five types clearly overlap and do not form a logically consistent pattern. Nevertheless, they describe some of the main ways in which research areas have been delimited. In practice a study of a particular institution may be connected with some felt problem, and problem-orientated research may test previously formulated hypotheses. Indeed, it is a mark of the increasing sophistication of social research that this is beginning to happen. Nevertheless, these five types will form a useful basis of classification.

1. PROBLEM-SOLVING RESEARCH

The problems defined vary with time and place and the persons concerned. The problem of a management may be how to prevent workers from restricting output. The workers' problem may be how to get the management to pay them what they consider a fair day's pay. If a fair day's work and a fair day's pay are defined differently by the two groups, as they may well be, each will see the problem as quite different. Each will call for a differently orientated piece of research, although both would be applied research. The academic theorist may well see, in their different definitions of the problem, a nice topic for research into a conflict situation.†

★See pp. 7, 8.
†Tom Lupton has an interesting discussion of such differences.[1]

In a country where poverty is a major problem, it can be a research topic. Where poverty is no longer a problem, the use of power in government, factory, and office may become a matter of practical as well as academic interest. Where a country is so poor that there is totally inadequate *per capita* income, the problem of poverty may well be one for research by the applied economist, concerned with increasing the national product or with the inequity of distribution of the world's wealth. In a country where productivity is increasing and one finds poverty in the midst of plenty, the problem is one concerning the student of politics, of administration, and of social structure, as much as it is of the economist. Thus the problem of poverty in India or Africa today is quite different from the poverty in which certain sections of the American population find themselves. The last case is much more like the problem of poverty in Britain in the late nineteenth century where extreme poverty existed amidst increasing plenty.

This was the problem which excited Charles Booth and which he set about studying systematically.[2] Booth started his study in a most practical manner. He ceased to share the value judgements of earlier times that "the poor were poor because they were poor", and began to conclude that poverty was not God-given, but was economically and socially determined. But what was poverty? How much poverty was there? Where was it to be found? These were questions that had first to be answered. Booth set about answering them by applying the principles that he would have used in his business life: find out the facts before you start making policy. Indeed, the fundamental principle of finding out the facts first is one which is still too little understood. Often one hears arguments about facts. Where the facts cannot be found, of course, one must argue and speculate. But why argue and guess when it is possible to go and find out? This was Booth's attitude, and it is one that is basic to all social research: find out the facts, collect the evidence, and then analyse it. After this you have a basis upon which policy can be made. The facts will not tell you what to do. They will tell you what the situation is and, given your goals, what there is to be done to achieve these goals.

This was the way Booth went about it. He aimed to find out the facts about poverty. His method was to ask the school board officers for a description of all the families, street by street, where they visited, and to report whether or not there was poverty there and what degree of poverty.

In order to measure poverty, Booth had first to define it.

> By the word "poor", [he says] I mean to describe those who have a fairly regular income, such as 18/- to 21/- a week for a moderate family, and by "very poor" those who fall below this standard, whether from chronic irregularity of work, sickness, or a large number of young children. I do not here introduce the moral question: whatever the cause those whose means prove to be barely sufficient, or quite insufficient for decent independent life. are counted as "poor" or "very poor" respectively: and as it is not always possible to ascertain the exact income, the classification is also based on the appearance of the home.[3]

His definitions and descriptions may look a little odd to us today, especially the weekly wages of the 1880's. The important point is that he had a definition of poverty. On the basis of this any family could be placed above or below the "poverty line". This is a useful concept of Booth's. The income defined as necessary for a "decent independent life" constituted the poverty line. Those with a larger income were above the line, those with less were below it, were in poverty. Thus not only did Booth measure poverty, but he showed how he had done it. Thus we know that there is a considerable likelihood of inconsistency in the categorization of particular cases because Booth relied to some extent on the subjective judgements of the interviewers about the amount of poverty in a home. As he says in the quotation above, "the classification is also based on the appearance of the home." What the school board officers thought about a family entered into the final count, and each officer might have a different opinion as to how to classify the "appearance" of a home.

This was where Rowntree, who also studied poverty and who followed Booth, made an advance on Booth's work.[4] Rowntree increased the precision both of the collection of the information and the application of the poverty line to the individual cases. This he did by two changes in Booth's method of working. First, he collected the information directly from the families concerned, using for the purpose interviewers employed and directed by himself, rather than Booth's method of using the reports of school board officers. Second, he gave a new precision to the definition of poverty leaving nothing to the judgement of the interviewers. His method was this. He ascertained "what income is required by families of different sizes to provide the minimum of food, clothing, and shelter needed for the maintenance of merely physical health". Rowntree's bare necessities were bare indeed, allowing nothing for such things as beer and tobacco or for what he called "the mental, moral, and social sides of human nature".[5] Thus Rowntree first made estimates of the minimum necessities of life in terms of how much food was needed and so on and then put a price on each of these. The weekly cost of his standard diet was as follows:[6]

Men	Women	Children 8–16	Children 3–8	Children under 3
3s. 3d.	2s. 9d.	2s. 7d.	2s. 1d.	2s. 1d.
Average for adults 3s.		Average for children 2s. 3d.		

This was based on the cheapest food it was possible to buy to give a diet which would include the following nourishment:[7]

Men		Women		Children 8–16		Children 3–8	
Cals.	Prots.	Cals.	Prots.	Cals.	Prots.	Cals.	Prots.
3560	137	2987	115·5	2738	87·2	1824	66·0

Having defined the standards so rigorously, Rowntree then proceeded to differentiate between primary and secondary poverty.

Those in primary poverty were those whose income, given the number in the household, was insufficient to achieve the standards indicated above. Those in secondary poverty, on the other hand, were those who would have had enough to achieve this standard "were it not that some portion of it is absorbed by other expenditure, either useful or wasteful".[8] It can be argued as Professor Moser does, that secondary poverty has a subjective base, but as he agrees primary poverty was more precisely defined.[9]

Rowntree's first study of poverty in York had been undertaken in 1901 and was revised in 1922. On the basis of his studies he published in 1918 a book on the minimum wage necessary for physical efficiency. This he revised in 1937, using the results of the British Medical Association's committee on minimum food requirements as the basis.[10] By this time, Rowntree did allow some small margin, under the heading of "sundries", for optional personal expenditure. This was the standard that Rowntree used in the late thirties when he resurveyed York, a study which was published in 1941 as *Poverty and Progress*.[11]

This was a valuable document because not only did it assess the extent and nature of poverty in York at that time, but also made it possible to compare the changes that had taken place since the turn of the century. Thus two "snapshots", or static accounts, of the situation in relation to poverty could be put together to gain some idea of changes over time.

Booth in his work had not only developed the concept of the poverty line but had indicated that at different periods a family might move in or out of poverty. Rowntree took the concept of the poverty line and applied it more systematically to the stages of the family cycle, showing how when a couple have young children the family tends to be in poverty: as the children start to work the family climbs above the poverty line. After the children have left home and when the breadwinner retires the family may again fall into poverty. Thus an individual may well be born into poverty, be above it in early adolescence, fall into poverty again when he has small children, and finally die in poverty.[12] Thus Rowntree showed that while he found 7230 persons in poverty at the time of survey, many more persons than this had been in poverty at some time of their lives.

After the initial contributions of Booth and Rowntree the next contribution of considerable importance was the introduction by Professor Bowley of the London School of Economics of the idea of the sample. Booth and Rowntree were both wealthy business-men. They had considerable resources at their disposal. Both used methods which involved taking counts of the entire population. This is lengthy as well as expensive. Bowley, a professor, had no such resources at his disposal.[13] He therefore devised methods of sampling whereby it is possible to assess the state of an entire population by the examination of only a section of it. Sampling will be discussed in greater detail later in Chapter 6.

The most recent developments in Britain have been to devise new methods for the assessment of poverty. These have sometimes been connected with national assistance payments on the assumption that the state gives in such aid what is considered the minimum necessary. Thus these scale rates are taken as the poverty line and any family who falls below this line is considered to be in poverty. On such bases attempts have been made to measure the extent of poverty today and to discover which groups of people are in poverty.[14] Notably the low income earner, the aged, the chronic sick, and the large family have been isolated as vulnerable. In addition attempts have been made to assess the adequacy of the national assistance scales to keep the recipients of benefit above the poverty line.[15]

Associated with this work and with comparative studies over time has come a clear understanding that poverty is a relative concept. It is relative to the wealth of the society in which it occurs and is therefore relative over space as well as over time. He who is counted poor in Britain today would be relatively affluent in the slums of Calcutta or the hills of Lesotho. Where the poverty line is drawn, below what level it is considered unreasonable to expect a man to live, that is to say who is called "poor", depends on the level of income of the rest of the population. This has led to an understanding that methods of measuring poverty such as those of Booth and Rowntree can only be useful in the short run and, as Lynes has said, "may be out of date before the work of computing it is complete".[16] Nevertheless, some standard must be taken in the short run on the general lines of the classical scholars of the field but such a standard is always relative to the place and the time in which it is applied.

Thus the study of poverty, an essentially practical problem, has been approached systematically in Britain for nearly three-quarters of a century. It has added considerably to our knowledge of society. It has done this in three ways. One, at the level of fact, it has told us how much poverty there is in the country at various places and at various times. It has also told us who are the people who suffer this poverty, when, and in what circumstances. Second, in measuring the extent and nature of poverty, advances have been made in the methods of social research: methods have been developed of collecting data directly from the people whom it is about; methods of sampling have been developed to reduce the burden and extend the possible range of research. In analysis, the development of concepts like the poverty line makes the data both manageable and meaningful. Third, the practical consequences of the work have been most extensive. An understanding of the circumstances under which poverty occurs has made possible the provision of measures to reduce it. The isolation of particular occasions of economic stress, such as childhood, old age, and sickness, has led to the provision of social security benefits to help meet these crises: family allowances, retirement pension, and sickness and unemployment benefit. Recognition of the importance of unemployment as a cause of poverty led to an understanding of a different kind: that it is impossible to eradicate poverty, nor, indeed, will a social security system work, unless the economic system can provide for full employment. Full employment itself removes the poverty due to unemployment and underemployment and makes possible the surplus to help in the other defined crises which lead to poverty.[17]

Surveys designed to solve practical problems have thus led to practical results in the shape of government policies. Nor have they been without theoretical interest and consequences. It is true that Booth did not relate his data to the social class system, but it is essential empirical data for anybody wishing to analyse that system. Nor did Rowntree in isolating his three stages of economic crisis relate his data to theories of the family cycle. Nevertheless, his analysis does point up one aspect of the cycle of the family and one which relates to the description given, for example, by MacIver 4 years earlier.[18] A combination of MacIver's theoretical description and Rowntree's particular and precise measurements led the author to analyse the Banbury family as a process which develops over time.[19] Similar analyses were developed in other places.[20] The point is simply to indicate that problem-oriented research may have theoretical implications however little the author may have taken account of theory. Such implications are likely to be of greater and more immediate impact if the relationships are made plain by the author himself. It behoves researchers therefore to relate empirically derived relationships to theoretical relationships wherever possible.

There are many other practical fields into which social research has been and is being done: the social aspects of planning; the sociology of housing; the problems of fertility and population control; the problems of management–worker relations; the problems of the organization of factories, hospitals, administrative offices. Many problems in applied research fall on the frontiers between two disciplines or involve contributions from a number of disciplines at the same time. Such kinds of research can be among the most difficult, but also when they are successful, among the most rewarding of the applied research projects.

One of the major difficulties in applied research is achieving understanding between the client and the researcher. The client may ask unanswerable questions and the researcher may be unable to communicate his results to the client who is not a specialist. The only answer to this problem would seem to be discussion and interaction between the two parties throughout, from the early planning of the research to the execution of the recommendations.

2. STUDY OF PARTICULAR INSTITUTIONS

The second general type of research is a study of a particular social institution or a particular aspect of the social structure. Sociologists have for many years been concerned with social inequality. This has shown itself in the concern for those in poverty as in the case of the reformers described above. It has appeared, too, in the concern of sociologists with the ways in which society is stratified: how it is divided into status or class groups or categories. General observation showed that some kinds of people felt themselves inferior or superior to, or the same as, other kinds of people. It also showed that people in the broad categories of "equals" tended to live in many respects the same style of life. Observation also showed that some people change their category in the course of their life, moving up or down these horizontally conceived strata. Here then was an interesting problem the solution of which would lead to a better understanding of society. How many strata were there? What were the characteristics of each? Who were the people who moved up and down? How many moved and in what direction?

There are numbers of ways of answering questions of this kind about a particular social process or social institution. One method was used shortly after the Second World War to try and answer just such questions by D. V. Glass and his colleagues. As Glass says in his introduction to their work which was first published in 1954 under the title *Social Mobility*:

> The programme as a whole is concerned with the processes of social selection and differentiation which are at work in Britain, with the formation of social strata, and with the nature, composition and functions of those strata. Such problems are central to the study of social structure; they are of direct concern both for the development of sociological theory and for the formulation of social policy.[21]

Glass and his colleagues wanted to start with the formation and structure of the middle classes, but before they could do this they had to undertake a general investigation of social status and social mobility in Great Britain. They therefore undertook a nation-wide survey

of this particular aspect of British society. They started with an empirical inquiry into the prestige popularly accorded to various occupations. Respondents were given a list of occupations which they were asked to rank according to the relative prestige they attached to each. On the basis of the opinions of respondents, in both a pilot and a more general survey, a classification of occupations was drawn up by Professor Glass's associates. Since this was a ranking of occupations, the social mobility subsequently measured is really occupational mobility, and is only social mobility in so far as the social ranking of the occupations relates closely to other forms of social stratification. There is evidence to show that occupations are closely connected with other social attributes. Nevertheless, there are clearly limits to the extent to which it is reasonable to infer social mobility from occupational mobility as Glass and his associates undoubtedly recognize. For present purposes we may limit ourselves to that part of the study which is solely concerned with the national study of occupational ranking. The inquiry was based on a stratified random sample of the entire nation (see Chapter 6 for a discussion of sampling). That is to say persons selected on a systematic basis throughout the country were asked a series of questions which were laid out on a carefully constructed interview schedule*
which is reproduced in full in the book.[22] The questions were designed to find out the age, sex, and marital state of the respondent, his education, his occupational history, and his parent's and spouse's occupations. The object was to discover how much people had moved up or down the occupational prestige scale compared with the position their parents held, and with the position they themselves started from.

There are other ways of finding out about a particular aspect of society than by a nation-wide questionnaire of this kind, and some of these, such as inquiries into particular institutions in particular places, were also used in this book to build up the general picture of social mobility. Thus this work, while it overlaps with problem-oriented research and uses more than one research method, is an interesting example of an attempt to study one process over a whole

*See Chapter 5 for a discussion of questionnaires and schedules.

society. The way it was done, first ranking all occupations and then seeing how people move about among them, assumed a uniform ranking and stratification system. This theoretical assumption has since been questioned.[23]

Studies of particular institutions or processes need not make such assumptions. They need not necessarily use the nation-wide schedule interview as a research technique, nor need they be restricted to one society or nation. The cross-national study by Lipset and Bendix into social mobility which followed the study of Glass *et al.* and other similar national studies in different parts of the world, are interesting examples.[24]

Further illustrations of the different ways in which a particular institution may be studied throughout a society may be drawn from the field of religious institutions.

John Highet has published two books on the churches of Scotland.[25] In the course of his first book (1950) he attempts to cover all the denominations and many of the sects that were represented in Scotland in the period after 1945, with a postscript correcting as far as possible the figures to 1949–50. In the course of his survey he not only presents such useful facts as the incidence of church membership, but also deals with the following broad topics: the principles, government, and strength of the main churches, denominations, and sects; what is called "the retreat from religion", where he considers the extent to which religion is declining or maintaining its position; he goes on to talk about "the gospel in action", by which he understands the active work the churches do, both in extending their own religious activities and in work in the wider society, in social services, for example. In a final section on "the mind of the churches" he deals with attitudes to a number of matters of Christian principle and practice, as seen by the various denominations.

In his later work, published in 1960, Highet attempted (as he says, p. 9) "a factual account, as full as time and resources have made possible, of certain aspects of the life, activities, and statements of the majority of Scotland's Churches in the mid-twentieth century, with assessments and opinions by churchmen and others and a few comments of my own". In order to supplement official records of church membership and to gather further information, Highet sent out a questionnaire to a sample of ministers of eight of Scotland's churches, and a similar questionnaire was sent to representatives of other denominations. In addition, certain selected persons were asked a larger range of questions some relating to opinions and attitudes. The range of topics considered is not dissimilar to that of the earlier work, although it is rather differently laid out.

The work of Bryan Wilson, *Sects and Society*[26] is yet another way of looking at religious institutions in a complex society. Wilson has not attempted to survey all religious groups in Britain, but has undertaken a specifically sociological study of three religious groups in the country. Wilson starts from the position that he accepts the hypothesis "that religious movements, as essentially social movements, can be expected to stand in specific relation to social classes, to their prevailing economic and social conditions, and to the cultural and social ethos obtaining within such social groups".[27] His principal methods of study were to use the published materials of the sects in question (Elim, Christian Science, Christadelphian), to solicit life histories, interviews, use informants and to undertake prolonged participant observation in one congregation of each movement. He was apparently able to check that these were not atypical congregations. What results from this approach is an understanding of these sects and an addition to various aspects of social theory about charisma, routinization, etc.*

Another approach to the study of a particular institution is to look at it in a number of different societies and different places. Thus the institution of marriage has been studied comparatively for many years.[28] One recent study was the work edited by Meyer

---

*"Charisma", literally "gift of grace", was used by Max Weber to describe the authority exercised by individual leaders who initiated new ideas and gathered social groups around themselves, in this case new religious groups. "Routinization" Weber used to describe the process by which such informal groups are transformed over time into formal organizations with a typical structure of office holders of various ranks.[30]

Fortes, *Marriage in Tribal Societies.*[29] Here studies of marriage in four different societies are presented. Three are ethnographic accounts in African tribal societies and the fourth is a re-analysis of Malinowski's data on the Trobriands. In his introduction, Professor Fortes makes it plain that new theoretical insights can still be gained from comparative studies such as these. He also shows that there is no hard line to be drawn between the institution in "simpler" and "more complex" societies. It is clearly most important that particular institutions, or particular social processes, should be studied both in detail within one society and also comparatively over a range of societies.

3. LOCALITY STUDIES

It is also interesting to establish the interrelations of one set of institutions to another within one society, to see its constituent parts, and how these are articulated to each other. Social anthropologists have commonly adopted this approach in the past in dealing with small-scale so-called simple societies. Thus they have been able to show the relationships among law, politics, economics, marriage, the family and kin, and the value systems of the societies they have studied. In practice, many monographs concentrate more on the analysis of one group or set of institutions than another. Nevertheless, these could be seen, in terms of the individuals and groups involved as well as abstractly, to be related to the total society. In highly complex societies this is much harder to do. This is one of the reasons for undertaking the third type of research mentioned, that is studies of particular localities.

In this kind of study a rural or an urban area is geographically delimited for analysis "in the round", the object being to see how the various aspects of the social structure and culture fit together. One of the most famous and the earliest attempt to do this, for a complex society, was the study in 1928 by the Lynds of the Mid-West American town they called Middletown and which they revisited and restudied later.[31] There followed in America the series of studies initiated by W. Lloyd Warner in the Yankee City

Series.[32] In England, since the Second World War there have
been studies of Gosforth,[33] Banbury,[34] Pentrediwaith,[35]
Westrigg,[36] and elsewhere.[37]

Although there are differences in approach, all these studies
cover aspects of the life of the locality such as the economic,
political, and religious structures, as well as the part played in the
total social structure by other associations, by family and kin and
by social stratification. All are concerned with interrelations
between some or all of these aspects of the locality. What is em-
phasized depends partly on the relative importance, in a given case,
of different aspects of the social system, but also on what the observer
perceives to be the important components of the local social system.
This depends on his personal bias, on the social position he adopts
in the area, or is placed in by local residents, and on the theoretical
framework he adopts.

These studies have used a variety of methods but all have one
technique in common, namely participant observation. That is,
the research worker goes to live in and join in the life of the society
which he is studying. This method will be fully discussed in
Chapter 4.

4. STUDIES OF INSTITUTIONS WITHIN LOCALITIES

There is a fourth type of study which should be mentioned at
this stage. This is a combination of the last two approaches. That is
to say a particular institution is studied in some detail in a particular
local context. This is true, for example, of Young and Willmott's
study of East London[38] and of Rosser and Harris's book on the
family.[39] In widely differing areas the object was the same: to
examine the particular institution of the family in one locality. A
charge is sometimes made against studies of one institution
on its own (those dealt with here under section 2) that misunder-
standings can arise because data are torn out of their social and
economic context. The hope is that by studying the institution in
a particular locality in association with other institutions, this
danger can be avoided. In studying social relations it is sometimes

the "minute and particular" rather than the "gross and general" which are important, as Meyer Fortes has remarked in another context.[40] Or, as Michael Banton has put it, "The sociological approach cannot do itself full justice in the absence of studies of inter-personal relations for they make the link between general social forces and everyday behaviour".[41]

As Banton suggests, these approaches are not mutually exclusive. It is essential to know what broad distribution of categories of people there are in the country at large and in the county of which the locality under study is a part. Without this type of data, which comes from the broad survey, one would have no idea where, on the spectrum of social forms, to put the particular case under consideration. The large-scale survey of a particular institution can provide information of a kind the local study cannot and without which the latter would be hampered. At the same time, local study can put flesh on the bones of the structural skeleton which the broad survey reveals. Sometimes locality studies are seen as microcosmic studies, thus Frankenberg refers to Banbury as a "microcosm", presumably of the macrocosm of British society.[42] The use of "micro" and "macro" to distinguish national from local studies is of limited help, because what is micro in one context is macro in another. Thus while Frankenberg may look upon community studies as micro studies, they are macro studies compared with the studies of small groups.[43] It is clear that the idea of macro and micro are in this sense relative, a matter of level, or perhaps to be looked at as a set of Chinese boxes, so that what may be seen as micro in one context is macro in another.

The study in detail of selected streets in Banbury was one example of this. As Frankenberg does, one can call the Banbury study a piece of micro-sociology when Banbury is looked at as a place holding a fraction of the British population. Once the frontiers of Banbury itself are seen as the boundary, the study of the whole town becomes the macro study and the study of individual streets becomes the micro study. Thus residents of a street could be classified on the national occupational scale employed by Glass and his associates in their social mobility study, and at the same time their inter-personal relations and style of life observed, giving a dimension that the study of nation-wide categories cannot give.

5. THEORY TESTING

The final type of study is that which aims to test a particular theory. In the past there has been a tendency to confuse social philosophy with sociological theory. Social philosophy is concerned, among other things, with what constitutes a better or worse society in some sense, with ways of altering an existing society towards a desired goal, and with ways of assessing an existing society in terms of such goals. Sociological theory, on the other hand, is not concerned with evaluation of this kind. It is concerned with a series of propositions which explain social relations and social processes as they are, and since they explain, can also predict. Explanation and prediction are the opposite directions of the same process. It is true that sociology does not have a set of highly abstract interrelated propositions, at least not in the sense that physics does. Nevertheless, there is a growing body of deductive and inductive propositions about a number of aspects of society. It is not really appropriate to refer to generalizations based upon empirical research as theory. Where such generalizations can be related to propositions with wider application, then one can be said to be moving towards a theory. Research set up to test propositions derived in such a way are likely to be of wider interest than those which relate to a single fieldwork situation.

Hypotheses, however derived, concerning the relation between two or more variables, must be tested in a situation in which "other things" can be controlled. This may be done by exercising direct control, as in a laboratory experiment, so that it is known that no external factors are contaminating the findings. Such control is not often possible in the social sciences. Towns cannot be built to test theories, and in this case attempts must be made to exercise control by such devices as cross-tabulation or by matching individuals or groups in all other respects than that being examined.

While theories relating to large-scale society can generally only be tested by the second approach, some theorists have attempted to test their propositions experimentally on small social groups. Thus, for example, Bavelas[44] developed certain theoretical propositions about communication patterns. His propositions were based on the geometric properties of different communication patterns, e.g. whether communications were passed around a circle, in a chain, or in a star-shape. He considered how groups organized to communicate in these patterns might actually function and showed that, depending on the pattern and the way it was operated, a group could solve a problem with varying numbers of messages being sent and expending more or less time in the process.

Having theoretically demonstrated that such differences existed, Bavelas then attempted to show by experiment the implications of these differences. His colleagues, Sidney Smith and Harold Leavitt, conducted controlled experiments in which groups of people were asked to solve certain problems, the individuals being arranged in cubicles, and able to pass messages to other members of the experimental team only through slots, so that the patterns of communication were determined by the experimenters. Smith's experiments showed that the individual in the most central position of the pattern was most likely to be a leader, and that those in the positions the furthest from the centre were most likely to have low morale during the work. These experiments have been followed by others. Harold Guetzow, for example, examined particularly the differentiation of roles in small groups[45] and Marvin Shaw introduced the factors of democratic and authoritarian leadership into various networks.[46]

Bales is another theoretician who has tried to test his theories empirically.[47] He conceived of interaction as a continuous process, and of all group activity as problem-solving. Therefore he considered that all behaviour, that is each individual act, which might in operation be a gesture or part of a sentence, could be fitted into some structural category. These categories he constructed deductively before starting his experiments. His theory rests on the assumption that in social interaction people like to be able to

predict the behaviour of others and will act to make this possible
or to release the tensions which develop in an unpredictable situation.
To test these ideas empirically, Bales developed experimental
techniques at the Harvard Laboratory of Social Relations. These
techniques will be discussed later.*

In such experimental studies of small groups the researchers may
in some sense be said to be dealing with analogies of the social
processes found in larger societies,[48] but their theories have not
been tested outside the laboratory. David McClelland provides an
example of someone who not only has tested hypotheses in a
controlled laboratory situation but also in larger societies.
McClelland started with an interest in motivation to achievement.[49]
He developed ways, by the use of suitable stories, of experimentally
arousing achievement motivation in subjects and of measuring the amount of motivation aroused. Later he saw a connection
between achievement motivation and large-scale economic
change.[50] He connected the socialization processes which instill a
desire for achievement into children, and the thesis expounded half
a century before by Max Weber in the *Protestant Ethic*.[51] Weber
associated protestantism with other worldly asceticism which led in
this world to hard work, the accumulation of unspent wealth, and
thus the rise of capitalism. McClelland's suggestion was that, for
reasons of their religion, Protestants had a high motivation to
achievement, and that this led to subsequent economic development
in countries with a high proportion of Protestants. To test his
theory McClelland set out to discover whether those groups or
countries which had demonstrably undergone considerable periods
of economic development had *before* that time exhibited in their
literature, folk-tales or school readers, a high interest in achievement.
This required an elaborate cross-cultural and international study.†
On the indices he used McClelland was able to demonstrate his
hypotheses showing, for example, that English literature before
the industrial revolution paid attention to achievement. He deals
similarly with ancient Greece, medieval Spain, and the United

*See pp. 66, 127–8.
†Some of the methods used are discussed later.   See pp. 45, 46.

States in the nineteenth and twentieth centuries, as well as with archaeological evidence and pre-literate peoples.

To sum up, five major types of research have been identified. The line between each is not hard and fast and many pieces of research contain elements of all the types. The types merely indicate what is the main motivation for the research. Type 1 was the unashamed attempt to solve a particular social problem. This kind of research is expected to reach conclusions on which action can be based. It is in some ways the most difficult kind of research to do, requiring a good deal of courage, because wrong conclusions are likely to show sooner or later. Nevertheless, it is very often the most unsatisfactory kind of research. In the past it has often been undertaken by people whose sociological training has been inadequate, so that these problem-oriented researches are miscellaneous and uneven in quality. Nevertheless, they should not be despised; after all, Durkheim built his theory of suicide on many isolated studies.[52]

The second type of research was concerned with examining a particular social institution or social process throughout an entire society or making comparisons over a number of societies. The third type of research was that which aimed at studying the inter-relations of social processes or social institutions in one rather narrowly defined locality. Such accounts were often largely descriptive, ethnographic accounts of a particular people, or a particular place. The fourth type was a combination of types two and three, that is to say a particular institution was studied in its place as part of a particular local society.

The fifth type, which some would say should be the only type of social research, was designed to test hypotheses derived from sociological theory. In fact such tests should be and usually are embodied in the previous three types. The object in separating this category is to point to types of research which have aimed at testing (a) theories of social interaction under controlled conditions, and (b) propositions of wide scope about major social institutions and processes.

REFERENCES

1. LUPTON, T., *On the Shop Floor: Two Studies of Workshop Organization and Output*, Pergamon, Oxford, 1963.
2. BOOTH, C., *A Survey of London Life and Labour*. For a full bibliography of the works of Charles Booth see T. S. and M. B. Simey, *Charles Booth: Social Scientist*, O.U.P., 1960.
3. BOOTH, C., The inhabitants of the Tower Hamlets (School Board Division), their condition and occupations, *J. Roy. Stats. Soc.*, 1887, p. 328. Quoted by T. S. and M. B. Simey, *op. cit.*, p. 184, for a discussion of Booth's definitions of poverty.
4. ROWNTREE, B. S., *Poverty: A Study of Town Life*, 1922 edition.
5. *Ibid.*, p. 118.
6. *Ibid.*, p. 136.
7. *Ibid.*, p. 134.
8. *Ibid.*, p. 118.
9. MOSER, C. A., *Survey Methods in Social Investigation*, Heinemann, 1961, p. 21.
10. ROWNTREE, B. S., *The Human Needs of Labour*, Longmans, 1937.
11. ROWNTREE, B. S., *Poverty and Progress: A Second Social Survey of York*, London, Longmans, 1941.
12. ROWNTREE, B. S., *Poverty*, 1922, p. 171.
13. ABRAMS, M., *Social Surveys and Social Action*, Heinemann, 1951, p. 44.
14. See, for example, D. COLE, and J. UTTING, *The Economic Circumstances of Old People*, Occasional Papers on Social Administration, No. 4, Codicote, 1962.
15. LYNES, T., *National Assistance and National Prosperity*, Occasional Papers on Social Administration, No. 5, Codicote, 1962.
16. *Ibid.*, p. 10.
17. *Beveridge Report*, H.M.S.O., Cmnd 6404, 1942.
18. MACIVER, R. M., *Society*, p. 199.
19. STACEY, M., *Tradition and Change: A Study of Banbury*, O.U.P., 1960, p. 134.
20. ROSSER, C., and HARRIS, C., *The Family and Social Change*, Routledge and Kegan Paul, 1965, p. 164.
21. GLASS, D. V. (Ed.), *Social Mobility*, Routledge and Kegan Paul, 1954, p. 3.
22. *Ibid.*, pp. 93 *et seq.*
23. STACEY, M., *op. cit.*, p. 144.
    KAHAN, M., BUTLER, D., and STOKES, D., *Brit. J. Sociol.* **17** (12), p. 124 (1966).
24. LIPSET, S. M., and BENDIX, R., *Social Mobility in Industrial Society*, London, Heinemann, 1959.
25. HIGHET, J., *The Churches in Scotland Today: A Survey of their Principles, Strength, Work and Statements*, Jackson, 1950.

HIGHET, J., *The Scottish Churches: A Review of their State 400 Years after the Reformation*, Skeffington, 1960.

26. Wilson, B., *Sects and Society: A Sociological Study of three Religious Groups in Britain*, Heinemann, 1961.

27. *Ibid.*, p. 4.

28. MALINOWSKI, B., Marriage, *Encyc. Brit.*, 1929.

    LOWIE, R., Marriage, *Encycl. of Soc. Sciences*, 1933.

    RADCLIFFE-BROWN, A. R., and FORDE, D. (Eds.), *African Systems of Kinship and Marriage*, O.U.P., 1950.

    PHILLIPS, A. (Ed.), *Survey of African Marriage and Family Life*, London, 1953.

29. FORTES, M. (Ed.), *Marriage in Tribal Societies*, C.U.P., 1962.

30. WEBER, M., *The Theory of Social and Economic Organization* (ed. T. Parsons), Free Press Paperback, New York, 1964, pp. 358 *et seq.*

31. LYND, R. S., and LYND, H. M., *Middletown: A Study in American Culture*, New York, Harcourt Brace, 1929.

    LYND, R. S., and LYND, H. M., *Middletown in Transition: A Study in Cultural Conflicts*, New York, Harcourt Brace, 1937.

32. WARNER, W. LLOYD, and LUNT, P. S., *The Social Life of a Modern Community*, New Haven, Yale Univ., 1941, Yankee City Series, No. 1.

33. WILLIAMS, W. M., *The Sociology of an English Village: Gosforth*, first published 1956, 3rd impression 1964, Routledge and Kegan Paul.

34. STACEY, M., *op cit.*

35. FRANKENBERG, R., *Village on the Border*, London, 1957.

36. LITTLEJOHN, J., *Westrigg: The Sociology of a Cheviot Parish*, Routledge and Kegan Paul, London, 1963.

37. FRANKENBERG, R., *Communities in Britain, Social Life in Town and Country*, Pelican, 1966.

38. YOUNG, M., and WILLMOTT, P., *Family and Kinship in East London*, Routledge and Kegan Paul, 1957.

39. ROSSER and HARRIS, *op. cit.*

40. FORTES (Ed.), *op. cit.*, p. 12.

41. BANTON, M., in his review of *Industrialization and Race Relations* (Ed. Guy Hunter) in *New Society*, 21 October 1965, No. 160.

42. FRANKENBERG, *op. cit.*, 1966, p. 14.

43. Cf. D. MARTINDALE, *The Nature and Types of Sociological Theory*, London, Routledge and Kegan Paul, 1961, p. 464, and I. WHITAKER, The Nature and value of functionalism in sociology, in *Functionalism in the Social Sciences*, Monograph No. 5 of the American Academy of Political and Social Science, 1965, esp. p. 132.

44. BAVELAS, A., Communication patterns in task-oriented groups, in *Group Dynamics–Research and Theory* (Ed. D. Cartwright and A. Zander), Tavistock, 1960, pp. 669 *et seq.*

45. GUETZKOW, H., Differentiation of roles in task-oriented groups, in Cartwright and Zander, *op. cit.*, pp. 683, *et seq.*
46. SHAW, M. E., A comparison of two types of leadership in various communication nets, *J. Abnorm. Soc. Psychol.*, **50,** 127–34 (1955).
47. BALES, R. F., *Interaction Process Analysis*, Addison-Wesley, 1950.
    For useful discussion of Bales' work see M. S. OLMSTED, *The Small Group*, Random House, 1959, pp. 117 *et seq.*, and J. MADGE, *The Origins of Scientific Sociology*, Tavistock, 1963, ch. 12.
48. This case is specifically argued by Bales, *op cit.*, but questioned by a number of theoreticians, notably C. WRIGHT MILLS, *Sociological Imagination*, O.U.P. (New York), 1959.
    See also OLMSTED, *op cit.*, p. 104.
49. McCLELLAND, D. C., ATKINSON, J. W., CLARK, R. A., and LOWELL, E. L., *The Achievement Motive*, Appleton–Century–Crofts, 1953.
50. McCLELLAND, D. C., *The Achieving Society*, Van Nostrand, 1961.
51. WEBER, M., *The Protestant Ethnic and the Spirit of Capitalism*, trans. Talcott Parsons, Unwin University Book, 1965.
52. GIDDENS, A., The suicide problem in French sociology, *Brit. J. Sociol*, **16,** 3 (1965).

CHAPTER 3

How to Start: Designing Research and Examining Documents

INITIAL READING AND RESEARCH DESIGN

Let us suppose that by now the area of research and the problems which are to be examined have been decided in broad outline. Before the research can begin there must be a research design. The process of research design is really a matter of increasing the clarity and precision of the questions to be asked and the ways of answering them. It is supposed that the researcher knows a good deal about his subject before having decided on the area of study and the broad questions. Nevertheless, having decided on these the first step must still be to find out as much as possible of what other people have said about the subject. Reading a research report with a view to further investigation has a surprisingly different perspective from reading for general interest. One is immediately concerned not only with what has been done, but what questions were formulated and why, and how the answers were arrived at.

The first thing to do therefore is to gain access to a good library and learn how to use it. For those in remoter places this may mean spending some time in a library centre before embarking on the fieldwork. If this is going to be an expensive business, allowance will have to be made for it in the budget. Inter-library or postal loan arrangements can be made with some libraries.

Having read all the relevant books and articles on and around the subject and refined the research topic in the light of this new knowledge, more detail can be put into the research design. What are going to be the main means of obtaining the information, of testing the hypotheses? There are a number of methods for the collection of primary data which are open to the researcher. He may ask questions, he may observe behaviour, he may make experiments. Generally speaking, sociologists either ask questions or observe behaviour in its natural setting. Except in small group studies the opportunities for experiment in society are limited. It is, for example, too expensive to build a new town in a particular way just to see the social consequences of so doing. The best one can usually do is to find a town which *was* built in that particular way and examine the social consequences it had.

Another difficulty is that there are generally so many factors involved in a social situation, in addition to those that one is interested in, that it is hard to disentangle them. If certain kinds of social behaviour are observed in our new town how are we to know that they were the consequences of building the town in that way? Might it not have been the time that it was built or some other exterior factor? One way around problems of this kind is to observe several new towns. If the social behaviour in question is found in all of them perhaps we can say that this behaviour, a high birth rate say, is associated with new towns. If X represents the new towns and Y the high birth rate and X always goes with Y in every case we take, we can say that there is probably a connection between them. This is not to say that there is a causal connection. There may well be an intervening variable. In this case it might be migration, or more particularly age at migration, which has made the connection between new towns and a high birth rate. Suppose it is young married couples who most commonly move to new towns, the birth rate is likely to be high simply because young married couples are more likely to have children than any other section of the population. Sometimes it is easy, as in this hypothetical case, to spot what makes the connection between X and Y. Sometimes it is less obvious. One useful question then to ask is: "X goes with Y, but can we find situations in which Y goes with non-X?" In this case, new-town birth rates, we might not find it for a whole town, but could find it for housing estates in old towns. Here again we might find we had a high proportion of young married couples and a high birth rate and this would incline us to the view that it was the young couples who were the factor leading to the high birth rate in the new towns. Thus, supposing we were concerned with the population structure of new towns, how we designed the research would depend on the aspects of the population which were of particular interest. If we just wanted the facts of the population structures of a new town, this can be simply measured, either from statistics already collected or by asking a sample of the population. This tells us nothing about social behaviour. As soon as we start asking questions about attitudes or behaviour our research design must be modified from a straight head-counting exercise. To understand whether a new town population is different, and in what ways, from an old town population requires a comparison between the two. To find out whether young couples in new towns behave differently from young couples elsewhere would require further comparisons. Young couples who go to new towns may be different not only from the rest of the population (as they obviously are by the definition of their age) but also in other ways. Thus one might want to compare them with young couples on new housing estates in old towns and with young couples in older areas of old towns. If young couples in all the new towns had characteristics in common which the young couples elsewhere did not share, then it might be reasonable to infer that there was some association between this behaviour (a high birth rate say) and the new town couples. It would, however, not be reasonable to conclude that it was living in a new town which made them behave in this way. It might well be that these young couples behaved like this (had more babies) for the same reason that led them to the new town in the first place. In order to clarify the relation between cause and effect a research design would have to include a number of questions about the motives for moving, attitudes about the ideal family size, and birth-control practices. Thus it is most important to work out quite clearly what are the research questions one wants answered and to design the research accordingly. It is equally important to realize what are the limits of the statements that it will be possible to make as a result of research designed in the way proposed.

The population which is to be the subject of the research must be decided, and other populations for control or comparison selected, if the researcher wants to be able to make statements about relationships which could not be based upon one population alone. Thus the statement "In this new town the birth rate is high" is meaningless by itself. The statement "In this new town the birth rate is high compared with the national average" can be safely made upon the basis of the thorough study of one town and available national birth-rate figures. Generalizations about the birth-rate "in new towns" could not be made on the basis of the study of one town only. Generalizations about the birth rate of young couples in new towns cannot be shown to have a connection with the fact of living in a new town unless the behaviour of other young couples, as controls or for comparisons, has also been looked at.

According to the subject of the research and the questions it is proposed to answer, so the method of collecting the primary data will vary. For some purposes it may be better to ask direct questions, for others to observe behaviour, and for others again to use a combination of both methods. Readers will be better able to judge what would be suitable for their research after reading the following chapters on the major methods of data collection.

SECONDARY SOURCES: EXISTING WRITTEN DATA

The process of design, as should be becoming clear, is one of acquiring increasingly detailed knowledge of what others have already uncovered and refining one's own plans. This can only be done within a broad overall research design, so that the details will form part of a coherent whole, against which the relevance of any projected activity can be judged.

In addition to books and articles there are nowadays many published facts, frequently in statistical form, about many aspects of society. So that, as indicated above, some pieces of research can be done entirely on the basis of secondary analysis of existing data. Thus, the first part of the hypothetical study of new town populations, described above, could be done from the population data officially collected for new towns. The later stages would require original research. Secondary analysis of existing information, assuming the original data were well collected, is by no means to be despised.* It is necessary to find out, before starting, what data exist, how reliable, and how relevant they are to the research topic. They may be held or published by the government body (local or central) or by private institutions, or in some cases private persons.

The illustrations of written documents, whether verbal or statistical, will be taken from British material. Students working in other countries will be able to find out whether comparable data exist there. They may find that they have access to data not available in Britain. Students working in Britain should still make their own inquiries, for the list given here is illustrative of the data available and does not pretend to be exhaustive. In any country the sensible thing, having exhausted what the library has to offer, is to go and ask those practising in the field. A director of education, for example, will be able to say what data are published and made publicly available by the central government or by his local authority on educational matters. This will provide a check on what the student has been able to discover in the library. He will also be able to say whether other relevant data is available in his files. For access to this, special permission may have to be granted. The chances of obtaining such permission vary from one place to another, with the degree of democracy in the area and the attitude to the spirit of free inquiry in general and to social research in particular. There are real difficulties of confidentiality when data relates to individuals and the authority may feel that it can only release the information when it has been made anonymous. This may involve the officials in work for which they cannot afford the time. Much always depends (a) on the local custom and law in these matters, and (b) on the degree of confidence that the research worker can inspire.

*Now that the data bank has been established at the University of Essex the use of appropriate retrieval systems makes it possible to undertake secondary data analysis of a kind new in Britain, although such centres are already in existence elsewhere in the United States and on the Continent.

OFFICIAL STATISTICS

For Britain one of the most comprehensive sources of data is the census. This has been taken every 10 years since 1801 with the exception of the 1941 war year. There was a quinquennial census in 1966 dealing, on a sample basis, with matters about which there was little rapid change, and including some questions not already asked.

The census involves an inquiry into certain facts about every member of the population. In Britain the head of each household is responsible for filling in a form for himself and all other members of his household. These forms are delivered and later collected by enumerators who have certain other responsibilities, such as helping the respondents complete the forms where necessary, making summary analyses, and so on. Each enumerator, who works under local census officers, is responsible for an area of about 200 households, known as an enumeration district.* All people in a household on the night of the census are enumerated in that household, whether or not it is their usual residence (which fact is recorded). Full details about the method of collection of the census are given in the introduction to the census reports.[8]

The information covered by the census and its method of presentation is also set forth at the front of each census volume. It includes information about:

(i) The sex, age, and marital status and relation to the household head of household members.

(ii) Birthplace, nationality, and whether this is the usual residence of the members returned on the form.

(iii) Occupation, industry and place of work, unemployment, sickness, part-time working.

(iv) Age at which education ceased, scientific and technological qualifications.

(v) Internal migration.

(vi) Marriage and children.

(vii) Ability to speak Welsh (in Wales and Mon. only).

*In 1966, since it was a sample census, the E.D.s were larger and more aried in size.

(viii) Dwellings, households occupying them, housing conditions, housing tenure, usual household size.

In 1961 not all of this was asked of everyone in the population. Questions about employment, place of work, status in employment, education, scientific and technological qualifications, usual residence and change and duration of residence were asked of only 10% of the population. The object of this was to reduce the cost and to speed the process. In fact the publication of the 1961 census in Britain was extremely slow. Tabulations were still appearing in 1966. The production of volumes for the 1966 sample census has been a good deal quicker. The U.S. census has for many years asked a larger range of questions and has produced its results remarkably quickly.

Censuses do, of course, vary in their degree of accuracy. Theoretically, on the subjects they ask about, they should provide complete data for the whole population at that date. The subjects provide the information about themselves and their families. The whole census depends on the accuracy of this information. Certain sections of the population, notably non-English-speaking immigrants, were underestimated in 1961.

Naturally the population does not remain the same from one census to another. Between censuses, therefore, the Registrar-General provides estimates of births, deaths, and marriages, and other vital statistics. He makes *Quarterly Returns* and publishes annually a *Statistical Review*.

In addition the Central Statistical Office publishes an *Annual Abstract of Statistics*, which is a useful first document to refer to to discover if numerate information exists from government sources on the subject of one's research. It covers aspects of almost all government activity and gives the source (which ministry or department, for example) so that there is at once an indication of where to go for more detailed information. It covers area and climate; population and vital statistics; social conditions; education; labour; production; retail distribution and miscellaneous services; transport and communications; external trade; overseas finance; national income and expenditure; home finance; banking, insurance, etc.; and prices. In addition it has an appendix showing the standard regions and conurbations used for statistical purposes and giving the standard industrial classification (which is also published separately).

The Office also publish a *Monthly Digest of Statistics* covering much the same data. An annual volume of *Regional Statistics* has recently been started giving information culled from official sources for each of the standard regions. Some of this information is not elsewhere available. For regional studies, or for local studies, it is useful to have the data gathered together in this form. The *Welsh Digest of Statistics* is an extract, for the Principality, of data relevant to that area. The Ministry of Labour *Gazette*, which is published weekly, is a major source of statistics about labour, wages, and allied subjects.

There was also for a time a body known as the Interdepartmental Committee of Social and Economic Research which published *Guides to Official Sources* between 1958 and 1961. It published six reports on: labour statistics; census reports; local government statistics; agricultural and food statistics; social security statistics and census of production reports.[9]

Local government statistics fall into three categories: those collected and published by the Ministry of Housing and Local Government; those collected and published by others, for example, the Institute of Municipal Treasurers and Accountants; and certain statistics published by each individual local authority on its own behalf. The latter vary from one authority to another, although there tends to be a common minimum of vital statistics from the local medical officers of health.

There are, in addition, certain sources of non-official statistics such as those provided by the London and Cambridge Economic Service, the Co-operative Permanent Building Society on national house price trends, and by special surveys such as that published for Town and Country Planning *Housing in 1965*.

There are an increasing number of publications dealing with international statistics such as those of the Organization for European Economic Co-operation (O.E.E.C.) and various organs of the United Nations: the United Nations Statistical Commission published in 1958 the *International Programme of Social Statistics* including the International Labour Office (I.L.O.) family living statistics and social security statistics; the Food and Agricultural Organization (F.A.O.) household consumption surveys; and the United Nations Educational and Scientific Organization (Unesco) basic facts and figures. The U.N. Bureau of Social Affairs has published three-yearly, starting from 1958, a report on the world social situation. The U.N. Statistical Office has published a compendium of social statistics at four-year intervals from 1963. They also publish the *Demographic Year Book*, while Unesco publish a series on population and culture.

There are three points to make about official statistics in general: (i) they only exist where some area of social life is controlled: thus until the United Kingdom started to control the inflow of Commonwealth immigrants there were no figures on this subject; (ii) it is essential to know the conditions under which the figures were collected and the definitions which were used. In particular in examining statistics over time it is important to notice whether the definitions have changed in that period or the boundaries of the area to which they refer been altered; (iii) the reorganization of government departments leads to certain changes: thus the annual report of the Board of Education became that of the Ministry of Education and now of the Department of Education and Science. More seriously, for studies of comparison over time, the results of departmental changes may include new methods of data presentation and breaks in a statistical series. In times of government reorganization difficulty may therefore be experienced in tracing data, and care should always be taken in this matter.

OTHER WRITTEN DATA

Apart from official records and statistics and the reports and returns of professional and commercial bodies which are published, there may well be other written records which are relevant to the subject in hand. Thus newspapers, periodicals, and popular journals are all sources of information and are themselves, as means of communication, objects of study. The more literate and affluent the society the greater is the problem of selection. Whether literary sources should be analysed must depend upon a strict test of relevance. Thus, in studying a particular locality, as well as looking at any written histories and examining central and local government material on the area, it would be sensible to look at the files of the local newspaper for the preceding and the contemporary periods.

An examination of newspaper reports may be essential to an explanation of the attitudes to a particular problem which is being examined. This, as Duverger[1] points out, may be particularly true in a study of political attitudes and events.* The role played by the "golliwog" in much children's literature may well be relevant to a study of the origins of colour prejudice in children. For some mothers what the magazines and the advice columns of the newspaper say about child-rearing and other matters may be an important influence on their behaviour. In other words, what would be passed from mouth to mouth as folk-lore in preliterate societies in literate societies may be communicated in print.

The test of relevance must be strict or the student will find himself overwhelmed by a mass of data. The technique of content analysis is one way round this difficulty (see Chapter 8). The documents in question may be examined for such factors as how much space they devote to a particular topic. The number of inches a newspaper devoted to the "teenage problem" at certain time intervals could be measured to get some idea of the extent to which this was felt to be a problem. Or one may use content analysis to note how often a particular attitude appears or a particular type of behaviour is advocated. Thus it would be possible to analyse children's literature to find out how frequently Negroes are portrayed as "bad men", how often as neutral, and how often as "good men". In non-white countries a similar analysis of children's tales could be made to show how often the "bad man" in children's stories was non-black.

*Although what is *not* said may also be most revealing as work being done on local papers by Alan Beith at Nuffield College, Oxford, is showing (unpublished thesis).

Children's stories as well as folk-tales and literature were analysed by McClelland and his associates to try and find out how much members of different societies were affected by achievement motivation.[1] Here the whole research depended on secondary analysis of documents. McClelland found that among less-advanced societies, those which had traders had more references to achievement in the folk-tales. He also found that where children's school readers contained achievement stories the country was at the same time making above-average economic advance. He also found that large numbers of references to achievement in a country's literature immediately preceded an upswing in that country's economic achievement.

PERSONAL DOCUMENTS

Letters and diaries constitute another type of written evidence which sometimes exists in advance of research being done. These can be valuable sources of information, particularly in the exploratory stage, but they present certain problems. It may be difficult, if not impossible, to prove their authenticity. This may be particularly so if the researcher calls for them publicly and pays for them.* They may be difficult, and certainly will be time consuming, to analyse. Diaries and autobiographies as sources of data may also be criticized because they are (a) written by people who are unrepresentative, and (b) they have been distorted in the writing, having been written with a view to publication or to impress any possible reader. Nevertheless, these criticisms could be made of almost any data which rely upon the author's own account of himself. Thus those who interview well may be as unrepresentative of the general population as diary writers.

Sometimes diaries or life histories are deliberately solicited by researchers at an exploratory stage of their research. This was done, for example, by Bossard and Boll[4] in their study of the large family system. They collected accounts from 100 persons who had

*See, for example, the discussion on the use of personal documents by Thomas and Znaniecki in the *Polish Peasant* summarized by Madge.[3]

been members of large families. They do not pretend that these data are statistically representative of the whole of the United States. However, this method provided some outline of the subject, and yielded hypotheses which could later be tested by more precise methods. Bossard and Boll used both written life histories and interviews. They found that the methods were complementary, sometimes the interview yielding more information, sometimes the written record. They specifically suggest that some people can write better than talk and vice versa.

The special problems in the use of personal documents for social research can be summed up in the two questions: "Are they genuine?" and "Of whom are they representative?" Documents including personal documents can be particularly useful when time and/or distance make the interviewing of respondents impossible. This was true of Shakespearean England, analysed by McClelland through its literature, and the achievement motives of countries scattered all over the world, analysed through children's readers.[2]

Personal documents can also be useful in the exploratory stages of any research. The researcher may not yet know what all the relevant factors are. If he went into the field at this stage with a formal questionnaire he might not obtain a proper account because he had left out one or more relevant factors. Diaries or letters which were already in existence, or life histories solicited by the researcher, will include all the factors which the writer thinks are relevant to his subject at the time and which he is able to express in words. What is included will vary from one person to another, although the researcher may guide the informant when soliciting life histories.

In all cases when using documents, whether those already existing or those especially called for, it is wise to cross-check the data from other sources by whatever means possible. Sometimes the data can themselves be checked, or other sources examined to see if they lead to the same general conclusions. Different sources leading in the same direction encourage one to believe that reliable data are being used even though such tendencies cannot constitute conclusive proof of accuracy or reliability.

KEY INFORMANTS

Another way of starting is to use key informants. This is the traditional method of the anthropologist, but as has been suggested sociologists may consult officials and experts. Key informants can be used in fields about which there are no official records and in places where no relevant records exist. A key informant is simply someone who, by virtue of his particular position in the society, knows a great deal about the subject of the research. It may be that his expertise is to know who knows, so that he refers the research worker to others more knowledgeable than himself.

There is no doubt that a few good key informants can tell a research worker a great deal about his subject and that hours of patient listening are well rewarded. It is also true that key informants can mislead a worker intentionally, or because their knowledge of the society is partial or biased.

It seems likely that the more complicated and segmented a society is, the more likely this is to happen, although it can occur in small and apparently less complicated societies.[5] While one informant can usefully pass the researcher on to others, it is important to avoid being caught up in a chain of unrepresentative informants. In segmented societies key informants will be different persons for different parts of the society. Commonly there is a division between male and female activities; if both of these are to be covered, informants of both sexes will be needed. In any case it is wise to have a number of independent informants and to check the stories of one against another. The people and issues that are not mentioned, that do not "exist" for any one informant, are a source of bias in his report. The presence of the bias may itself be of great importance to the research. Professor Firth advocates the use of the questionnaire, in the anthropological field situation, at a late stage in the research simply to check on the representativeness and completeness of the data that has been collected from key informants.[6]

There is no easy way of advising how to find key informants. They may not be the persons who present themselves obviously. Thus the person whose job it is to welcome strangers to the village may not be a leading person in the village. Commonly a key informant is likely to be a leader in some sphere or other, or may be simply one who has been around a long time and knows the affairs of the place well. Views differ about the use of "marginal men" as informants. Such people often present themselves as informants. Their peripheral position has often made them more conscious than persons occupying central positions in social groups of the structure and processes of their society. Their views and experience may, however, be peculiarly idiosyncratic.[7]

In many circumstances there are formal organizations and the incumbents of certain formal offices are the obvious persons to use as key informants both because they have the knowledge and because their office makes them the acceptable persons to consult. In such cases it is necessary to check among the rank and file as to the status and acceptability of the officer concerned and to balance the official view with the many popular views.

To sum up: key informants are invaluable in helping to define and understand the problem in the early stages, but exclusive reliance should not be placed on what they have to say. Key informants should be drawn from more than one area of the groups to be studied.

REFERENCES

1. DUVERGER, M., *Introduction to the Social Sciences*, Allen & Unwin, Minerva, London, 1964.
2. MCCLELLAND, D. C., *The Achieving Society*, Van Nostrand, 1961.
3. MADGE, J., *The Origins of Scientific Sociology*, Tavistock, London, 1963, pp. 55 *et seq.*
4. BOSSARD, J. H. S., and BOLL, E. S., *The Large Family System*, Univ. of Pa. Press, 1965.
5. See for examples—O. LEWIS, *Life in a Mexican Village: Tepoztlan Revisited*, University of Illinois Press, 1951; and A. GALLAHER, Jr., Plainville: the twice-studied town, in A. J. VIDICH, J. BENSMAN, and M. R. STEIN, *Reflections on Community Studies*, Wiley, 1964, p. 297.
6. FIRTH, R., *Malay Fisherman: Their Peasant Economy*, Kegan Paul, London, 1946, Appendix 1.

7. VIDICH, A. J., discusses sympathetically the role of the marginal informant
    in "Participant observation and the collection and interpretation of
    data", *Am. J. Sociol.* **60,** 357 (1954–5)
8. In addition there is now a valuable review: BENJAMIN, B., *The Population
    Census*, SSRC, Heinemann 1970.
    In general the SSRC series 'Reviews of Research', of which this is
    one, should be consulted.
9. Since 1968 the Central Statistical Office have published quarterly *Statistical
    News: Developments in British Official Statistics.*

CHAPTER 4

Observation

THE methods of observation used in the social sciences fall into two main groups; participant and non-participant. In the former case the observer joins the group he is studying as a member and attempts to be at one and the same time one of the observed as well as the observer. In the second case the observer is where his subjects are but is not one of them and is not joining fully, and perhaps not at all, in their life. In some cases, as that of observing through a one-way screen, the subjects are not even aware that they are being observed or, if aware, are not disturbed. This method is sometimes employed by psychologists, watching children at play, and has also been used by sociologists in the study of small groups. In most cases of direct non-participant observation the observed are aware that they are observed.

In practice it is often not possible to draw a hard and fast line between participant and non-participant observation, for two reasons. One, the research worker may use both methods at once, and two, the participation is almost always partial, the difference lying principally in the amount of participation sought or achieved.

PARTICIPANT OBSERVATION

This is the name which was given in 1924 by Eduard C. Lindeman in *Social Discovery* where he criticized the questionnaire method saying: "If you wish to know what a person is really doing, watch him."[1] Participant observation may be open or concealed. That is a person may go to work in a factory (say) for research purposes and not reveal that that is why he is there. Or he may apply for a job saying openly that he is going to do research on the workshop relations in the factory while he is working there.

As well as being either open or concealed (of which more will be said below),* participant observation may be undertaken in the researcher's own culture, in a sub-culture of his own culture, or in an alien culture.

Schwartz and Schwartz, in "Problems in participant observation", define participant observation as "a process in which the observer's presence in a social situation is maintained for the purposes of scientific investigation".[2] This definition would rule out much of the participant observation in one's *own* culture which as Vidich recognizes is basic to all social research in that society. As he says: "Those who have worked with structured techniques in non-Western societies and languages will attest to the difficulty encountered in adjusting their meanings to the common meanings of the society investigated, a fact which highlights the extent to which the sociologist is a participant observer in almost all his work".[3] In drawing up questionnaires in one's own society one is in fact calling upon a good deal of knowledge gained simply by being a member of that society. Unwitting biases may be introduced for the same reason.

PARTICIPANT OBSERVATION IN AN ALIEN CULTURE

It is instructive to look at what Malinowski said about participant observation in an alien culture in *Argonauts of the Western Pacific* (1922). His aim was to study the trading system of the south-west Pacific. Malinowski complained (a) that the research worker's understanding of village life and of the myths and ideas of the people was "mangled by being forced into pidgin English", and (b) that most white residents, whether missionaries or traders, were inadequate as informants, because they rated cheaply, or treated with frivolity, "what is really serious to the ethnographer". On the basis of his experience in the field, in addition to having "real scientific aims", he stressed the importance of two other principles of method.

*See pp. 56, 58.

The first was that the inquirer should "put himself in good condition of work, i.e. in the main . . . live without other white men, right among the natives".[4] His third principle dealt with the application of certain special methods.

Here we are concerned with the principle of participant observation, although Malinowski did not use those words to describe the procedure. Malinowski considered that, while it was useful to have a white man's compound as a refuge in time of sickness or as a base for stores, it should not be near enough to fly to at any moment for recreation. The research worker should "seek the native for company". In this way, Malinowski said, "you become familiar with his customs and beliefs far better than when he is a paid, often bored, informant." After having a white investigator living among them for a while Malinowski believed the "natives cease to be interested or alarmed or made self-conscious" and the investigator ceased "to be a disturbing element". Malinowski stressed the value of having to learn how to behave by the "breaches of etiquette" that he made. For Malinowski the danger of a survey was that it presented the skeleton without the flesh and blood, and from documents he felt you could not get what he called "the imponderabilia of actual life".

As well as living in the village he suggested that sometimes the ethnographer should "put aside camera, notebooks and pencil" and "join in himself in what is going on". He can take part in the natives' games, he can follow them on their visits and walks, sit down and listen and share in their conversations. These "plunges" are most important for understanding in his view. Inevitably to pursue this method, it is important to speak the native language. Finally, Malinowski stressed how important it was "to grasp the native's point of view, his relation to life, to realize *his* vision of *his* world".

Malinowski was working out the principles of participant observation in what Barnes has described[6] as the "colonial period" when, as he says, "informants and other actors in the ethnographic picture were given their real names, even though some of their actions might be described in Latin, whereas nowadays informants and others are given disguised names but their actions are described in plain English". "Even Malinowski", Barnes says, "despite the tremendous changes he brought about in fieldwork methods still regarded the Trobriands as though it was a laboratory".

Writing a quarter of a century later on the fieldwork methods he used in Malaya, when investigating their peasant fishing economy, Raymond Firth also extolled the importance of direct observation. This was the only way to see "the full complexity" of "the present structure and functioning of social and economic relations".[6] Firth recognized that the research worker "is primary recorder as well as secondary collector and analyst". Firth weighed the advantages and disadvantages of the anthropological technique. Two drawbacks follow from the short period of study (one to two years). First, the full meaning may not be grasped and, second, temporary conditions may be mistaken for normal. In addition there are three dangers of bias. The first arises from the overweighting of the opinions of congenial informants. The second may come from the theoretical background of the researcher, and the third from the data which he selects. Firth's remedy to overcome the danger of not grasping the full complexity of the situation was to concentrate for months on a small community of about 1000 people, breaking off occasionally for rapid comparative surveys of an extensive kind. To avoid the dangers of mistaking the temporary for the permanent he used documents, the accounts of others, and the memories of the inhabitants.

The advantages that Firth saw in direct observation are similar to those suggested by Malinowski. Thus, Firth claimed as an advantage of the method that after 3 months' probationary period of living among the people and learning their language he "comes to see the community life in all, or nearly all, its aspects". He can see and trace the gaps. Firth stressed that the presence of the observer is an experiment in itself, just as Malinowski stressed the importance to him of the mistakes he made in learning the etiquette. Like Malinowski, Firth stressed the limits to the knowledge of local Europeans, mentioning in particular their lack of systematic knowledge about detailed aspects of the social and economic life which are important to the investigator. Firth, again like Malinowski, recognized the importance of language, and stressed the importance of using the vernacular throughout.

Firth indicated the need to check the facts given by local informants in order to eliminate any bias or inaccuracy they may introduce. He suggests that here is the place for the use of a questionnaire applied to numbers of the people. He recommended that this should be used and drawn up towards the end of the research and not at the beginning. In effect he advocated the use of key informants in the exploratory stage of the investigation to be followed later by more extensive, numerate studies of the whole group. (See previous chapter.)

Firth made a further important point concerning the value of team-work in studies using participant observation as a main method. In his case the team was a husband-and-wife one. His community was made up of Moslems who segregate women from men quite extensively. Firth therefore worked among the men while his wife worked among the women.[7]

PARTICIPANT OBSERVATION IN A SUB-CULTURE OF ONE'S OWN CULTURE

A classic example of the use of participant observation in a sub-culture of one's own culture is that of William Foote Whyte in *Street Corner Society*.[8] Whyte studied a poor, largely Italian immigrant part of a town in America, "seeking to build a sociology based upon observed interpersonal events".[9] Whyte found a number of factors important to the success of the method. First among these is personal acceptance by key individuals who will then introduce the investigator as *persona grata* to his friends and associates. The introduction should come from a member or members of that group. Such introductions lead to the acceptance of the research worker on the assurance of a trusted group member. To reach such a person it may be necessary to go, as Whyte did, through an intermediary. In Whyte's case this was a social worker.

Whyte found it better to make explanations of what he was

doing to the leader, rather than to all members of the group, leaving it to the leader to explain to the group members. This finding is one that may be modified depending on the size and complexity of the groups to be studied. Explanations to leaders are probably always important because without their co-operation the research is unlikely to be able to proceed. In large-scale studies further explanation may be needed throughout the research process at all levels and in all parts of the society, as new groups are encountered. The leader's agreement and understanding can serve as an introduction to these further groups, but more explanations are likely to be necessary.

Whyte relied on what Tom Harrisson[10] has called "overheards" rather than on questioning respondents very much. "If people accept you, you can just hang around and you'll learn the answers in the long run without even having to ask the question."[11] Whyte also found that although he was accepted as "one of them", he did not have to "play their game all the way". While to join at all in the games of the Trobriands was a revolutionary exercise for Malinowski, clearly he did not "play their game all the way" and remained separate and distinct, a man who took some of his recreation in ways strange to the "natives".

The limits of Malinowski's participation were perhaps more visible to the natives than they were to him. In Whyte's case, because of the common areas of culture, he was acutely aware of subtle differences and felt originally that he should behave as the gang behaved. He was a member of the gang but had the role there of social investigator. Gang members felt that if he adopted certain of their ways of behaviour this was out of keeping with his role. They knew, because of the common cultural areas, that people like Whyte did not behave like that. They therefore preferred him to maintain his own behaviour beyond a certain point, thus preserving the differences between them, maintaining his identity as social researcher and their identity as gang members.

Whyte found that as an accepted member of the group he had to take a role in an organization. Ronald Frankenberg also found that he was put into roles in organizations when he was studying in

Pentrediwaith on the borders of North Wales.[12] He was made an official of the football club and was asked to take the chair at meetings. It was inevitable that Frankenberg and Whyte should accept these roles in order to retain the good will of the people being studied. In both cases it helped the researchers to a better understanding of their subjects.

The extent to which the presence of the observer alters the research situation is a serious consideration. In Whyte's case not only did his presence increase the gang in numbers by one but, since they knew why he was there, in some ways gang behaviour was altered. This is perhaps most clearly shown by the gang leader's increased self-consciousness as when he complained: "You've [i.e. Whyte] showed me up plenty since you've been down here. Now, when I do something, I have to think what Bill Whyte would want to know about it and how I can explain it. Before I used to do things by instinct."[13]

PARTICIPANT OBSERVATION IN ONE'S OWN CULTURE

Participant observation in one's own culture may be in a formal organization, for example a factory, or it may be in a particular geographic area or in a particular social institution.

IN A FORMAL ORGANIZATION

An example of participant observation in a factory is given by Tom Lupton in his study *On the Shop Floor*.[14] Lupton used open participant observation because he felt it was wrong to spy. Also, the co-operation of both the management and trade union officials was necessary in the collection of documents and records. The present author would agree that for practical as well as ethical reasons, participation should normally be open.

Lupton was aware of the dangers of his own bias entering into the recording and analysis of the data. He therefore describes his own activities and states of mind, explaining that he was brought up among industrial workers, and was in the 1930's apprenticed as a marine engineer. In this job he learned the influence of customary workshop standards, the meaning of words like "tear-arses", "scroungers", and "bosses man", before he was trained as a sociologist and before, therefore, he could be a participant *observer*. Lupton knew that output was regulated and had seen and understood this as a worker himself. He shows how his theoretical orientations influenced his analysis. While studying sociology he became interested in the Bank Wiring Room studies[15] and was considerably influenced by these studies, but he felt that "investigators were University men working in active collaboration with the management of the firm. Research activities were accordingly directed to problems defined by management—or jointly by managers and research workers."[16] He thus shows how the values of the investigator influence the method of approach and conclusions (p. 17), pointing out that the phrase "restriction of output" carries an odour of disapproval and rests upon management goals and norms. Lupton therefore prefers to speak of "the behaviour of workers in relation to output".

The effect of using the technique of participant observation was to limit the study to two workshops in 2 years. Lupton justifies this by saying that what he needed was a first-hand description of behaviour and not a collection of statements about attitudes. He was concerned with a study that was focused on a social process.

Among the difficulties of participant observation he mentions, first, the lengthy preparation that is needed to establish relations with workers and managers and to establish confidence in the integrity and impartiality of the research worker. Second, he stresses how important it is to see managers and trade union men and shop floor representatives. None of these can be left out. Third, he draws attention to the amount of time spent in explanation, when in the workplace. Unlike Whyte he did not find explanation to the leaders was adequate. Fourth, he records the pressures upon the observer to take sides on occasions of divided opinions and how important it is that the research worker should resist such pressures. This is another aspect of the pressures which led Whyte and

Frankenberg to take office, and thus in a sense to take sides. Frankenberg as a stranger was asked to take the chair and thus also the
responsibility for decisions in order to *prevent* division in the group
of Pentre people who had cast him in this position. Similarly,
Whyte's office fell upon him because his personal attributes (connected with clerical skill) made it possible for him to perform a
particular service for the group. To take sides in an industrial
situation in which there are latent real conflicts would seem to be
another matter. In certain circumstances, of course, it may not be
possible to bridge the management–worker division as Lupton
apparently was able to do. Thus Karsh, in his *Diary of a Strike*, is
quite frankly giving an account of the trade union side.[17] This is
what he was concerned to do, and in the case of open conflict
undoubtedly he alone could not do otherwise.

Finally, Lupton discusses the problems involved in showing that
one is not a management man, not a trade union man, but that one
is a social investigator. This is a point to which many writers on
participant observation come back: the only role to adopt is the
honest and open one of social investigator. This is a difficult role to
fulfil because most people have little idea of what the role is. The
investigator therefore has to demonstrate it by his behaviour as his
study proceeds.[18]

IN A LOCALITY

Since 1930 there have been a number of illustrations of the
application of techniques similar to those developed by anthropologists like Malinowski and Firth (described earlier in the chapter),
to villages or towns or parts of towns in complex societies.[19] One
which uses these techniques, Frankenberg's study of Pentrediwaith,
a village on the North Wales border, has already been mentioned.
The first and by now classical study of this kind applied to a town
was the study in the 1930's by the Lynds of Middletown, a town in
the Mid-West of America followed some years later by a second
study, *Middletown in Transition*.[20] A study of a similar kind in
Britain was that of Banbury for which the fieldwork was under-

taken in the period 1948–51.[21] Here participant observation was not the only method used; indeed, among others the traditional random sample survey was an important source of data. But participant observation was a main method, without which the facts collected by other methods could not have been interpreted nor a synthesis reached. The method of participant observation in Banbury was the technique which supplied the data with which private troubles could be related to public issues in Wright Mill's phrase.[22] Data from participant observation made it possible to relate detailed inter-personal behaviour, social group behaviour, categories of people, and the broader economic and political structure together into a coherent whole.

In Banbury the research workers lived in the town and made their whole life there for the period of the research, only making such excursions from it as would any immigrant in similar circumstances, for visits to kin, for holidays, and any excursions occasioned by their work. Coming from other places, much appeared strange to them, and they learned about local customs by unintentionally breaking them, as has been described for the study of alien cultures.* In so far, however, as many of the ways of behaviour and beliefs were the same as those with which the research workers had been brought up, or to which they had become accustomed in the course of their lives, this particular advantage was less obvious than in the study of an alien society. Against this, less time was wasted in the initial stages in understanding the bare outlines of the local arrangements.

Nevertheless, due to the heterogeneous and segmented character of the contemporary society of which the town was a part, there were many customs and values strange to the research team. Furthermore, because of this segmentation it was not possible for

*It is most important for a participant observer to record all such breaches of etiquette or accidental breaking of taboos systematically in a note book. He should here include also all those occasions when he was about to say or do something but refrained because he picked up hints, "subliminal cues", which restrained him. This last process probably occurs more often in studies of one's own culture than major blundering errors.

one research worker satisfactorily to study the whole of the town by the methods of participant observation. Whyte reported difficulties in participating in opposing gangs. We have already seen that in Malaya the fact that Mrs. Firth, as a woman, was able to move freely among the women, was a great help in a society where the division between the sexes is marked, as it is among these Moslem people. Similarly, in Banbury no one person could study the whole of the town by methods of participant observation, not only because of the sex differences, which are important, but also because of social class and allied political differences.

In the team of three people studying Banbury there were research workers of both sexes and who, in their social origins, had come from the titled upper, the middle, and the working classes. They were able to exploit these characteristics in the interests of the research, each participating in a different sector of the town's life. In some sectors they moved about where their own origins made them acceptable, where their knowledge of the mores was a useful entrée. In other sectors they deliberately moved in areas of the society which by reason of upbringing were quite unfamiliar to them. In addition each research worker joined in whatever aspects of the life of the town interested him, be it sport, drama, religion, or politics. Each, because he was "in" one series of groups, was "out" of others. It is not only in formal membership of political parties or religious denominations that membership of one excludes membership of another. It is also true of many other areas of social life as well as, obviously, of the economic. One cannot be an employer and an employee, or at least not of the same firm, at the same time. Since this is so, any one researcher would not have been able, by participant observation, to report upon any more than a segment of the society. But, having three workers each joining in a number of spheres, the major ones of which related to the major social divisions, it was possible to put the pieces together. All the workers met together, usually at weekly intervals, sometimes more often, and exchanged information.

Thus the picture of the town which emerged, and which, further abstracted, was described in *Tradition and Change*, was a view of the town which no one worker could possibly have reached. This is not to say that it was therefore complete. Aspects of the town were not studied. Life inside the factories, workshops, and offices was not looked at at all. Only the relations of the work area to other social areas outside the workplace were dealt with. This was for reasons of time, money, and practicability. Doubtless certain other areas were missed altogether. This is to be expected in studying a complex and highly segmented society.

The necessity of co-operation between research workers able to move about in different parts of the society is seen even more clearly in the study by Davis and Gardner in *Deep South*.[23] The colour–caste line in the southern states of the United States of America could not at that time (1936) by definition be crossed. In order to see Deep South "whole" the only way in which it could be studied was for white and coloured workers both to be employed, each working on one side of the colour–caste line. While in Banbury it was possible for the research workers to meet each other in town to compare their research findings, it was not possible for the Davises and the Gardners to do this. They had to meet to exchange information outside the town. Once again, however, we are given a picture of Old City in Deep South, which none of the inhabitants of the place could possibly have. In much of Lloyd Warner's work[24] one has the impression that the participation was by "upper middle" class people moving about largely in the upper and upper middle areas of the localities studied. Consequently, the description of the "lower" classes appears less convincing than that of the upper. This would seem to apply also to the Deep South study and ideally one would have wished for a two- or three-person team on each side of the colour–caste line, so that the class differences could have been as well reported as the caste differences were.

Undoubtedly, in any particular research there will be limits to the areas in complex societies which can be studied. It will not always be possible to employ enough people for long enough to cover all the segments of the society. Where possible the major segments should be covered if a picture is wanted of the whole. At the very least it is necessary to understand enough of the total structure to know what limits must be set upon the observations made. Karsh, in the *Diary of a Strike*, was clear that his was an account from the side of the union, although he had a good deal of documentary evidence to show what the company's position was and took account of this in his analysis and his report.

The dangers of generalizing from an individual position in society are well known. The experiences of any individual are in some senses unique. There is no doubt that an individual's position will colour research to some extent, whether at the level of what is selected for observation or inquiry, what is perceived, or how it is interpreted.[25] In all kinds of research the individual social position should be self-consciously recognized, where necessary efforts should be made to counteract the biases it leads to. Since some social position is always held there is also a case for exploiting the very disadvantages of such involvement. Since social research workers can never altogether stand outside their work, there is a case for using their involvement for research purposes. This, in fact, is the theory which lies behind participant observation.

Such involvement can also be useful in studies where participant observation is not a main technique. Kirk's study of adoption is an example of this.[26] A simple question in a mailed questionnaire about outsiders being unfriendly towards adopters or their children produced an overwhelming majority who said they had not encountered unfriendliness. There was no prima facie reason to doubt this result. Kirk doubted it on the basis of his own experience as an adoptive parent. Discussion with groups of other adoptive parents and a consequently reworded and more sophisticated question* lead to the discovery of the different way in which outsiders view adopted from natural-born children. Kirk used his own involvement to uncover facts which might otherwise have remained hidden.

Participation of this kind is not initially engaged in "for the purposes of scientific investigation"[27] any more than the Davises and Gardners could control their skin colours, but being engaged in,

*See pp. 82–3 for further discussion of this.

the social position can be used for purposes of scientific research. Each research worker should clearly analyse for himself his research motivations and actions in terms of his social position, both past and present.* This is probably more relevant for social research than an experience of psychoanalysis, which has had such a vogue among some American sociologists.[29]

NON-PARTICIPANT OBSERVATION

As can be seen from the discussion above, the term "participant observation" should be limited to that method of observation in which the observer shares as fully as possible the life of those he is observing. It seems that some writers tend to think of participant observation as being direct observation without systematic recording and non-participant observation as being that which is systematically recorded. It is better to relate the definition to the degree of participation and deal with the recording methods separately. Schwartz and Schwartz in their study of a mental hospital do not make clear whether they were fully participant in the life of the ward (adopting the role of nurse, patient, or attendant) or to what extent they were simply present in the ward as direct observers of events there. One assumes they did not share the patient's illness, but as we have seen there are always limits to the extent to which the observer can be like his subjects. According to the Schwartz definition the participant observer role may be an integral part of the social structure or largely peripheral to it.[30] One assumes theirs was the latter.

In a study in Swansea† of children in hospital, two methods of direct non-participant observation were used, differing in their methods of recording and in the subject of observation, but neither being participant observation. In both cases the fieldwork was the responsibility of Mrs. Roisin Pill. Mrs. Pill's work was connected with the social consequences of the hospitalization of pre-school

*Lewis Coser's analysis of Simmel's position is an interesting model.[28]

†Undertaken in 1966 in the School of Social Studies of the University College of Swansea, with money from the Ministry of Health.[39]

children, specifically with the social interaction in the ward. In the first case Mrs. Pill used direct observation for exploratory purposes. She sat in a children's ward and recorded everything she could about the social interactions of the children, in a descriptive manner. From this she was able to develop certain tentative hypotheses for later testing, as well as to understand the general conditions which prevail in such a children's ward. The central part of her study was concerned specifically with the hospitalization of children for tonsillectomy. Again two methods of direct observation were used. Mrs. Pill followed all her subjects through their hospital stay, being present at certain crucial points (admission, day of operation, etc.) and also covering all types of period (e.g. times of day, visiting times, non-visiting times, etc.). These data she recorded in a diary which was concerned with the quality, as well as the relative amounts, of interaction of the children with certain defined categories—doctors, nurses, parents, other children, ward maids, etc. This method, although systematic, does not yield data which can be subjected to statistical analysis. Therefore, Mrs. Pill also used a more statistically based type of direct observation, known as time-sampling. Time sampling methods were developed by child psychologists in the 1930's for the observation of children.[31] With the assistance of others the relevant child cases were watched during all their waking hours. The universe which was sampled was their nominal waking day (7 a.m. to 7 p.m.).* This was divided into 20-minute intervals, during 5 minutes of each of which the child's interaction was recorded in detail, each period of 5 seconds during that time being recorded separately. Figure 1 shows a record sheet. This method of recording concentrated on the time spent and told little about the quality of the interaction. More was learned about this by the diary method. The "hard" observations provided by the time sample were an excellent check on the more non-statistical and qualitative data.

Clearly, in the case of a study of children participant observation is not possible. Sadly perhaps, no research worker can temporarily return to his childhood for scientific purposes. Also, where the

*See Chapter 6 for sampling methods.

subjects are very young children, the method of asking questions may not be thought appropriate. For these reasons some form of direct, non-participant, observation may be the best way to achieve first-hand data on social interaction.

Even though the observer is not participating in any role except that of observer in the ward life, the possibility remains that his presence may affect the situation. The child is aware that he is being watched, as are the parents, the nurses, the matron, and the medical staff. Some alteration of behaviour is likely. One can only hope that a consistent "act" cannot be kept up indefinitely for an extended period of observation. Indeed, evidence is that after a time the observer is to some extent "forgotten". This problem has been avoided by psychologists in their study of children's play in some cases by the use of a one-way screen, as was mentioned at the beginning of the chapter. For observation of children in their natural habitat or in school or hospital, as opposed to a test situation, such an apparatus is not, generally speaking, practical. When a screen is used the children are unaware that they are being observed.

In other cases they may be very little aware that they are being observed. The Building Research Station[32] in an investigation of the use made of children's playgrounds in housing developments, also employed a method of direct observation. Unlike the hospital study, in the playground observations were not directed to particular static children observed by one person each. They were directed to the playground, the number of children coming in, and what they did there. Not all of the children will have noticed that an observer was making records. These records were also made on a time-sampling basis, the numbers and activities of the children in a particular playground being recorded for a given time interval.

The direct observation of adults in a normal situation has also been undertaken. Several studies have been made in the factory setting. Lupton worked himself in the factory, but in other cases, notably the famous Hawthorne experiments, and in Glacier Metals, workers were observed directly by observers present in the room, whom they knew to be present. In the Relay Assembly Room study of the Hawthorne series the presence of the observers apparently affected the girls' output, so that the rate of work increased throughout the experiment.[33]

Another classic study of small groups by direct non-participant observation is that undertaken by Lippit and White under Ralph Linton's guidance.[34] Here children were gathered together into clubs which were lead by adults playing different kinds of leadership roles, "democratic", "authoritarian", and "*laissez-faire*". The adults knew all about it and were told what to do. The researchers observed through peep-holes and recorded activity and conversation. This was direct non-participant observation in an experimental setting.

Bales, in the studies mentioned earlier,* uses one-way mirrors and electronic recording apparatus, in experimental observations of small groups at the Harvard Laboratory.[35] The subjects are gathered together in a room designed for a discussion meeting and are watched from the adjacent observation room. A one-way mirror makes it possible for the group to be observed but not to be disturbed by the observer, both rooms being sound-proofed. The conversation of the subjects is relayed to the observation room and is also recorded for future reference. Observers record interaction on a moving tape as it takes place according to Bales's twelve categories. The moving tape makes for greater speed and accuracy. The sound recording makes checking and further analysis possible.

Participant observers may, of course, sometimes adopt the role of direct non-participant observer in relation to a particular event or series of events in the society in which they are participating. The observer is a participant in the larger society, but not in the group he is at present observing. Thus Firth describes going down to the beach to observe the fishing boats coming in and to record their catches. He was a participant of the fishing village, but not on these occasions of the boats he was watching return and unload. Firth in this connection also stresses the importance of systematic and careful recording of the observations and shows the records that he made of the catches.[36]

*See pp. 29, 30.

RECORDING

There is sometimes a tendency to confuse the system in the events recorded with the system in the records made. One of the disadvantages of participant observation is that the observer may not be present at all of a series of events because his group leads him elsewhere. On the other hand, the events he can observe may not be part of a series. Thus, by chance, one may be present at a crisis which is revealing of the social process and by misfortune not be present at another. Crises, by their very nature, are not regularly occurring events. However, a crisis at which a researcher is present may be recorded in a systematic manner, including in every case all the relevant data: the location, the numbers of persons involved, their social positions, the nature of the crisis, etc. Direct observation of regularly recurring events can be done systematically over time and also recorded uniformly. Such observations and recordings can be made alongside participant observation, as Firth made them. Whyte discusses in some detail his method of recording.[37]

CONCLUSION

We may conclude that there are circumstances in which participant observation may be a suitable main method, but that it can usually benefit from being augmented by questionnaire methods, as well as by other observational techniques. There are other situations in which, as with children, participation and questioning are both inappropriate, and non-participant observation must be used if one wishes data collected directly from the subject of the study. This may frequently have to be supplemented by questioning others about what they think is happening to the subjects. Undoubtedly, whatever is the main method used, other methods should often be introduced as checks or supplements. Thus Vidich and Shapiro, in comparing participant observation and survey methods, show the different value of each method and conclude: "The survey provides representative information which is given meaning by the anthropological observer [they mean the participant observer]. Frequently, but not always, survey methods may be used to test hypotheses developed out of the less formal experience of the observer. . . ."[38]

REFERENCES

1. Quoted by J. MADGE, *Tools of Social Science*, Longmans, 1965, p. 131, and by P. V. YOUNG, *Scientific Social Surveys and Research*, Prentice Hall, 1947, p. 122.

2. SCHWARTZ, M. S., and SCHWARTZ, C. G., Problems in participant observation, *Am. J. Sociol.* **60,** 344 (1954–5).

3. VIDICH, A., Participant observation and the collection and interpretation of behaviour, *Am. J. Sociol.* **60,** 355 (1954–5).

4. MALINOWSKI, B., *Argonauts of the Western Pacific*, Routledge and Kegan Paul, 1964 (first published 1922), Introduction.

5. BARNES, J. A., Some ethical problems in modern fieldwork, *Brit. J. Sociol.* **14,** (2), 118 *et seq.* (1963).

6. FIRTH, R., *Malay Fishermen: Their Peasant Economy*, Kegan Paul, 1946, p. 307. 2nd Revised ed., Routledge & Kegan Paul, 1966.

7. FIRTH, Rosemary, *Housekeeping among the Malay Peasants*, 2nd Edition L.U. Athlone Press, 1966. For a more recent discussion of anthropological field work methods see J. BEATTIE, *Understanding an African Kingdom:* Bunyoro, Holt, Rinehart & Winston, New York, 1965.

8. WHYTE, W. F., *Street Corner Society*, Univ. Chicago Press, 1955, Appendix.

9. *Ibid.*, p. 358.

10. Discussed by J. MADGE, *op. cit.*, pp. 137–8.

11. WHYTE, *op. cit.*, p. 303.

12. FRANKENBERG, R., *Village on the Border*, Cohen & West, London, 1957; and *New Society* **23,** 22 (1963).

13. WHYTE, *op. cit.*, p. 301.

14. LUPTON, T., *On the Shop Floor: Two Studies of Workshop Organization and Output*, Oxford, Pergamon, 1963.

15. ROETHLISBERGER, F. J., and DIXON, W. J., *Management and the Worker*, Harvard Univ. Press, Cambridge, Mass., 1939.

16. LUPTON, *op. cit.*, p. 4.

17. KARSH, B., *Diary of a Strike*, Univ. of Illinois, 1958.

18. For a further comment on the problems of observational study in a formal organization see P. M. BLAU, The research process in the study of the dynamics of bureaucracy, in P. Hammond (Ed.), *Sociologists at Work: Essays on the Craft of Social Research*, Basic Books, 1964, p. 16.

OBSERVATION 69

19. For example, C. ARENSBERG, S. T. KIMBALL, *Family and Community in Ireland*, Cambridge, 1948, and W. M. WILLIAMS, *The Sociology of an English Village: Gosforth*, Routledge and Kegan Paul, London 1964.
20. LYND, R. S., and LYND, H. M., *Middletown: A Study in American Culture*, Constable, London, 1929; and *Middletown in Transition: A Study in Cultural Conflicts*, Constable, London, 1937.
21. STACEY, M., *Tradition and Change: A Study of Banbury*, O.U.P., 1960.
22. MILLS, C. W., *The Sociological Imagination*, O.U.P., 1959.
23. DAVIS, A., GARDNER, B. B., and GARDNER, M. R., *Deep South: A Social Anthropological Study of Caste and Class*, Chicago, 1941.
24. WARNER, W. LLOYD, and associates, *Democracy in Jonesville*, Harper, New York, 1949.
25. See J. MADGE, *op. cit.*, pp. 119 *et seq.*, for a useful discussion of this point. It is, of course, the general argument from which Weber insisted on the essential difference between the social and the physical sciences and is at the basis of *Verstehende* sociology.
26. KIRK, H. D., *Shared Fate: A Theory of Adoption and Mental Health*, Free Press of Glencoe, 1964, esp. pp. 53 *et seq.*
27. SCHWARTZ and SCHWARTZ, *op. cit.*, p. 344.
28. COSER, L. (Ed.), *Georg Simmel*, Prentice-Hall, 1965, Pt. I, p. 29.
29. For an early discussion of psycho-personal bias see W. F. OGBURN, *On Culture and Social Change*, Phoenix, 1964, Chap. 23, 1922, p. 298.
30. SCHWARTZ and SCHWARTZ, *op. cit.*, p. 344.
31. See H. G. WRIGHT, Observational child study, in P. H. MUSSEN (Ed.), *Handbook of Research Methods in Child Development*, Wiley, 1960, for a review of the relevant literature.
32. HOLE, V., *Children's Play on Housing Estates*, National Building Studies Research Paper, No. 39, H.M.S.O., 1966.
33. ROETHLISBERGER and DIXON, *op. cit.*
34. LIPPIT, R., and WHITE, R. K., An experimental study of leadership and group life, in G. E. SWANSON, T. M. NEWCOMB, and E. L. HARTLEY, *Readings in Social Psychology*, Henry Holt, New York, 1952, p. 340.
35. BALES, R. F., *Interaction Process Analysis*, Addison-Wesley, 1950.
36. FIRTH, *op. cit.*, pp. 314 *et seq.*
37. WHYTE, *op. cit.*
38. VIDICH, A. J., and SHAPIRO, G., A comparison of participant observation and survey data, *Am. Sociol. Rev.* **20**, 33 (1955).
39. STACEY, M. (Ed.), DEARDEN, R., PILL, R. and ROBINSON, D., *Hospitals, Children and their families*. Routledge and Kegan Paul, 1970 (forthcoming).

CHAPTER 5

Asking Questions:
Questionnaires, Schedules, and Interviews

SOME behaviour is difficult to observe because it takes place in private. There are circumstances which it is quicker to ask about, when the answers seem likely to be reliable, than it would be to observe. People's beliefs and attitudes may be important and interesting to know, but they cannot be seen, because they are not behaviour, and they are rarely written down, so that they cannot be found in documents.

In such cases the best way of finding out is to go and ask people. Sometimes it is possible to ask just a few people, and this may be very important, especially at the initial exploratory stage of investigation. In this case, and at this stage, the use of key informants can be valuable. Their uses were discussed in Chapter 3. It is rarely satisfactory to rely entirely upon a few informants. Their information needs to be checked. In a population which is too big for everybody to be asked, a sample survey may be necessary. How a sample is drawn and certain problems involved in sample surveys will be discussed in the next chapter. First it is necessary to consider what kind of questions to ask and how to go about asking them. This is the subject of the present chapter.

People may be asked questions by post, on the telephone, or face to face. Telephone interviews are used to some extent in the United States but are of only limited use in countries in which the bulk of the population do not have a telephone in their home, and this still includes Great Britain. Postal inquiries have certain features to commend them. Where it is necessary to question a few people who are widely scattered geographically, there is a good deal to commend a postal inquiry. Such an inquiry has the advantage that it can be filled up at the respondent's convenience. It has the disadvantage that it may never be filled up at all. It seems likely that postal inquiries should be limited to certain kinds of people, for certain subjects, specifically to inquiries from the more highly literate about matters of which they have some specialist knowledge.

It is true, as Bossard and Boll point out, that some people can answer questions with pencil and paper who cannot answer them verbally.[1] The opposite is also true. Ideally perhaps one might wish to use both methods. Time and money rarely allow this, and the best method for the job in hand must therefore be sought.

For interviews of large numbers of the population, including persons of varying levels of literacy, it is probably most satisfactory and certainly most common to use the personal face-to-face interview.[2]

"The principal application of the interview in social science", as John Madge says, "is its use for the purpose of making people talk about themselves."[3] As such, interviews for social research purposes have certain distinguishing characteristics. The most important of these is perhaps the fact that the interviewer is a supplicant dependent on the good will of the respondent. Where a man wishes to buy a commodity and another has that commodity to sell, there is some mutuality of need on both sides. Where a client comes for advice to a doctor, social case worker, or other expert, he is the supplicant. In some cases he may offer money in return for the advice he receives: in others he may receive the services free. A research interviewer is in the position of the supplicant. He is doing the interviewing, but the information which the respondent has, and which the interviewer wants, he wants for himself and for his purposes, not for the respondent's interest or purposes. It may be arguable that the results of the research, in the long run, may help people in a similar position to the respondent, but, they are unlikely to be of immediate help to the respondent in his present condition. Indeed, he has not asked for any help. It is the interviewer who is asking for the help. For this reason it is useful to preface a research interview by the question "Can you help me?" It sets the relationship from the beginning. Apart from encounters with the police, and then within certain legal safeguards, it is only in the census that in Britain respondents are required by law to answer the questions asked of them. To force respondents to reply would in any case be likely to defeat the objects of the research, since if respondents really do not wish to answer they will simply lie to cover what it is they do not wish to reveal. An honest refusal will distort the results of the research less than a lying response, for the latter may be most hard to detect.

The aim of any research interview, therefore, is to get truthful information from people on a subject about which they are under no obligation to tell, if they do not wish to. How does one go about it? To ask for their help has already been suggested as an opening. To explain exactly what the study is about is also important at the beginning of any interview. That is to say they must be told what the research is about in language that they can understand. Technical language is essential to any subject for rapid and precise communication between its students. Any statement in such technical language must be capable of translation into common speech. The general aims of any research can be put into ordinary language quite simply and understandably for the consumption of laymen, who will include those very used to dealing with words as well as those whose trades have encouraged the development of other kinds of skill. It may be possible to persuade people to part with information for inadequately explained reasons or to mislead them once, but the respondents may discover that they have been duped and will react badly in the future to the same and to other research workers. It is against the best interests of the research to lie to respondents or to over-persuade reluctant respondents.

Goode and Hatt[4] examine the interview as a process of social interaction. They stress the need to learn to recognize the subliminal cues, those which are below the threshold of normal perception, through which we gain insight into a social situation. Researchers, they say, should learn to "read" such subliminal cues, and make them conscious. They can compare their "hunches" with those of others, and try systematically to check the predictions made from these hunches. It is the reading of such subliminal cues which leads the participant observer to avoid breaches of etiquette, and to recognize "taboo" areas without ever actually trespassing.* Goode and Hatt warn that the subject as well as the interviewer has insight and responds to the interviewer. How he dresses, behaves, appears, his facial expression will all affect the interview outcome.

Goode and Hatt then suggest that friendliness (rapport) must be established between the interviewer and his subject, but the interviewer must also command respect from the subject for his professional competence.†

When questions are being asked of a large population the researcher will not himself be able to interview all the selected respondents who may be scattered over a wide geographic area. If he tried there would be a considerable time lag between the first and the last interviews which might materially affect the results. Answers should be gathered within as short a time as possible. Otherwise external factors connected with the passage of time may make the data invalid.‡ Whenever the number of interviews to be undertaken runs into hundreds, extra people are usually employed as interviewers to talk to people on behalf of the chief researcher. Interviewers are very important in any large-scale survey. Although not responsible for the research design nor for the analysis that will follow, interviewers are those upon whom the most important work of collecting the data rests. Upon these data the whole study must depend.

*See previous chapter, pp. 52, 53, 59n.

†In this connection the interviewer is wise to carry an authority to interview.

‡An example of how drastically time may affect a sample I once came upon in "mopping up" after a survey had been completed. For a particular reason an attempt was being made to reduce the number of non-contacts about a year after the original sample had been drawn. The non-contact was a woman. She had not been contacted, as we learned, because she had already died at the time she should have been interviewed leaving a widower. Since the date of survey the widower had remarried and died leaving his second wife a widow at the address of our sampled woman.

Where interviewers are to be employed they must be trained, not only in how to fill up a specific interview schedule, but in the facets of interviewing described by Goode and Hatt as well. They must learn not only techniques of this kind, but the professional standards involved, e.g. when a respondent is promised that what he says is confidential it must really be kept confidential. They will be told that once they have handed the data to the research office any names or addresses will be replaced by a code number, so that the many people who may handle the information in punch rooms and computation laboratories will be unable to identify any person.

The length of time involved in training interviewers for any one survey can be considerable. For this reason most establishments, which regularly do surveys, keep a file of people they have previously trained and found suitable. Some kinds of surveys call for more sophistication and finesse than others. Nevertheless, a considerable minimum of skill is always required.

Because of the importance of the subliminal cues mentioned earlier, and of the researcher gaining a first-hand understanding of the limits within which he can trust the answers to the questions, the survey director himself may wish to do a certain amount of the interviewing. This can be more difficult than it sounds because as soon as an army of interviewers is employed there are considerable administrative problems which are likely to keep him tied to his desk all day. Those who wish to learn how to interview should first seek employment as interviewers on someone else's survey. Those who want to learn how to undertake a complete piece of field research are advised to start with something which is small enough for the researcher to do his own interviewing, before they add the problems of large-scale organization which immediately follow the employment of interviewers. Therefore, conducting a large-scale survey should be the third step in learning how to do research of this kind.[5]

TYPES OF INTERVIEW

Interviews may be divided according to how structured they are. In a *structured interview* all the questions are decided precisely in advance. There is no hard and fast dividing line between the structured and the unstructured interview. They should be seen as two ends of a continuum. In between the completely structured interview and the completely unstructured one fall a whole range in which varying degrees of control are exercised by and over the interviewer. A *structured question* is one where the way in which the question is asked, as well as the subject of the question, has been decided in advance. Every interviewer will ask the same questions in excatly the same words of every person they interview. An *unstructured question* is one where the interviewer is told to ask about a particular subject but is not given the form of words to use. An *unstructured interview* is one where the interviewer is simply given the subject of the whole interview in broad terms and left to elicit the information in any way he sees fit. Unstructured interviews are less likely to be comparable from one respondent to another and from one interviewer to another, but may elicit information that a more structured set of questions would not. Such interviews clearly demand more skill of the interviewer, who must have a clear understanding of what he is about, than does a structured interview. A *non-directive interview* is probably the most extreme form of the unstructured interview. The interviewer's object is to get the respondent to talk and to keep him talking, the subject of the interview as well as its form being largely left to the respondent. This form of interviewing is most commonly used for therapy, its use for social research being limited.[6] Still unstructured, but more formal, is the *focused interview* where the interviewer has a list of questions or topics he wishes to cover, but the way in which he asks the questions is largely left to his discretion. This kind of interview is particularly useful where experiences, feelings, reasons, and motives are involved.[7] Unstructured interviews are most common at the exploratory stage of any research and in those studies where depth of understanding is more important than large-scale coverage. At the early stage of any research a rigidly structured set of questions might well fail to ask all the appropriate questions because their relevance had not yet been seen. The strict comparability of one interview with another is less important at this stage than is the need to gather information about all the factors which are likely to be relevant. Once the exploratory stage has been passed in any study where statistical precision is important, a *structured questionnaire* or schedule is ordinarily used.* This is one in which the form of all the questions and the order in which they are set out are predetermined. Ordinarily these questions are written down on printed or mimeographed sheets.

There are certain clear advantages to the structured schedule. It ensures that all respondents have the same questions put to them and that the same form of words is used in every case. Although it cannot be assumed that every respondent will understand the same thing by the questions, it does reduce the differences which result from the use of varied words. Where a large number of respondents is involved, therefore, and where a number of interviewers are used, it is common to have all or part of the schedule following a common structure in this way. This is not to say that among these structured questions may not also be included subjects for freer discussion.†

*There is a case for retaining "questionnaire" for the mailed set of questions and using "schedule" for the set of questions that is to be administered in an interview. This usage is followed here, but since it has not yet become universal, questionnaires being sent through the post will be differentiated as *mail* questionnaires.

†Problems sometimes arise where the *form* of the words must be varied to the social category of the respondent, although the *meaning* of the question is essentially the same. Since "spouse" is not a word in common usage some schedules may contain many questions of the kind. "What is your husband's/wife's occupation?" "When did you last see your husband's/wife's father?" In some inquiries the subsequent questions may become quite complex, depending on the sex of the respondent. Here there is a case for preparing two schedules, one for men and one for women, as David Robinson of Swansea University College recently pointed out to the workers on the second Banbury study. They found that adopting this practice made it much easier for interviewers to put the appropriate question to the respondent and

The questions which are predetermined may also be divided into those which are *open-ended* and those which are *closed*. In open-ended questions respondents are free to reply to the questions in any way they wish. In closed-ended questions they must reply in one of a predetermined number of ways such as "yes", "no", or "don't know". In cases of collecting opinions or attitudes respondents may be offered a statement such as "Harold Wilson is a good Prime Minister" to which they are expected to say that they "strongly agree", "agree", "undecided", "disagree", "strongly disagree". Or respondents may be asked to indicate which of five income groups their earnings fall into. The advantage of closed-ended questions of this kind is that the responses can be pre-coded. Whether or not the data when collected are going to be processed by machine, it is necessary to code all the answers. This means dividing them into categories which are clearly defined so that they cover all responses and do not overlap with each other. For ease of analysis, particularly where the data are going to be put through a mechanical sorter or into a computer, these groups are each given a code number. Thus in the examples above there are five categories. In the first example the following coding might be used:

1. Strongly agree
2. Agree
3. Undecided
4. Disagree
5. Strongly disagree

In the second example the five income groups would be divided and numbered 1, 2, 3, 4, 5. In dividing up something like age or income, which are in fact continuous in that probably there is someone with

---

reduced the amount of paper needed for the schedule since there was no need to print alternative questions. Robinson had been faced with a similar problem in addressing two comparable sets of questions to mothers who had had under-five-year-old children in hospital in the last 12 months and to those who had never had an under-five in hospital. By providing his interviewers with two interview forms, one for the "hospital" and one for the "non-hospital" mothers, he reduced greatly the possible sources of confusion and misunderstanding.

every age you can mention and somebody has every odd sum of income, it is important not to be ambiguous about where the division between the categories falls. Thus if you write an age scale as:

> 0– 5 years
> 5–10   ,,
> 10–20   ,,
> 20–25   ,,
> etc.,

it is impossible to know into which category you are expected to put people age 5, 10, 20 and so on. It is much better to write:

> 0– 4 years
> 5– 9   ,,
> 10–14   ,,
> 15–19   ,,

In the case of money, one might divide income thus:—

> 0 and less than £10
> £10 and less than £20
> £20 and less than £30
> etc.

As long as one is clear in advance what categories are needed, precoding has many advantages. It saves time in analysis and encourages unambiguous responses. It is always wise to have a double check. Thus, it is well to ask people "What is your date of birth" and have the interviewer write this in as well as precoding into the relevant group. This method has two advantages: (i) it acts as a check on the interviewer's accuracy, and (ii) if the data is wanted for another purpose, for which the precoded categories happen to be inappropriate, it is possible to go back to the original schedule and recode the data in the new way.

There are some circumstances in which this safeguard must be abandoned because other considerations are more important. Sometimes respondents are willing to say into which income group they fall, or to indicate this on a card which is shown to them, when they are not prepared to reveal their precise income. In this case a better response may be achieved by using pre-coded groups and asking the question "Would you mind telling me to which income group you belong?" rather than asking "What is your income?"*

While the pre-coded reply to a structured question encourages an unambiguous response, it has the disadvantage that replies may be forced into a pattern that they do not really quite fit. It leaves no room for the "yes-and-no" kind of reply. In answer to the question about the Prime Minister there is no room to say "Well it depends what you mean by a good Prime Minister" or "Well, up to a point but . . ." so that a partial agreement may be recorded as "undecided" when the respondent is quite clear and quite decided, but neither agrees nor disagrees with the statement. Similarly, the "don't know" category in a yes/no/don't know set of responses will include those who really don't know, those who can't be bothered to think about the question just now, and those who know very well but who perhaps for that very reason cannot say clearly "yes" or "no".

It may be that for the particular research it is more important to divide people into categories, on one side or the other of a mythical line, than it is to record all the finer shades of differences. In that case forcing the decision may be the best in the circumstances. Where the finer shades of meaning are important this method would be inappropriate, and it would be wiser to ask an open-ended question. In our example they would be able to qualify their answers and explain their reasons for their views.

The disadvantage of open-ended questions is that they produce a mass of different answers, some using different words and meaning the same thing, and some using the same words and meaning

---

*In considering what categories to use consideration should always be paid to making these comparable with other researches and other sources of data. See pp. 139–40. In addition it must be pointed out that in a recent paper Elizabeth Gittus[8] has warned of the many hazards involved in collecting income data.

different things. Open-ended questions are often necessary, particularly in matters to do with beliefs and feelings, but they present a
problem for analysis. The methods of content analysis can be
applied to them, adding up how many times a particular point is
made. Content analysis will be discussed briefly later.* Selltiz *et al.*[9]
summarize the way to decide between open and closed questions
thus: closed questions should be used where alternative replies are
known, are limited in number, and are clear cut. Open-ended
questions are used where the issue is complex, where relevant
dimensions are not known, and where a process is being explored.
We should add that the open-ended question is always more trouble
and therefore slower and more expensive to analyse than the closed
question. The closed question may merely produce a stereotyped
response. So may the open question in the hands of an unskilled
interviewer.

DRAFTING A QUESTIONNAIRE OR SCHEDULE

When the form of the interview and the nature of the questions
including whether they should be open or closed, has been decided,
the first draft of the schedule can be prepared.[10] The order of the
questions should be decided by the way in which it might be
possible to conduct an ordinary conversation on the subject and
not by the logic of the inquiry. This point is well made by Goode
and Hatt in their section on carrying the interview forward.[11]
This means that topics may be widely separated in the schedule
which the research worker will want to put side by side when he is
analysing the results. This does not matter. They can be brought
together when the data is being tabulated. What is important is
that the questions should flow naturally and follow one another as
they might in an ordinary conversation.

Thus if one has started by explaining the nature of the research
the first question should be one which the respondent can see to
be connected with the subject of the research as it has been explained
to him. At the same time it should be a question which is not

*See pp. 125–7.

likely to give offence. It also helps if it is straightforward and easy to answer. Remaining questions are then grouped as naturally as possible, leaving until the end of the interview any that are likely to give offence to some people. Having already answered so many questions, respondents may well be prepared to answer a final one or two rather "personal" questions, which might have shocked them at the beginning. Also, if they are not willing to reply to these questions it is better that their refusal should come at the end, and relate only to these questions, rather than at the beginning. One question which offends at the beginning may lead to a refusal to answer the whole schedule.

This first draft should then be circulated to colleagues and any other willing persons one can find for their criticisms and comments, as to ambiguous questions and so on. Thereafter it should be amended in the light of these comments and a draft produced which can be tested in the field in a pilot study. With this must also be prepared the interviewers' instructions giving definitions and explaining how to answer questions, fill in pre-coded responses, and so on. The interviewers should then be trained and sent out with the pilot. When they come back the following moves must be made: (i) to ask them about any difficulties they may have encountered; (ii) particularly about any ambiguities or resistances which may lead to inadequate or misleading responses; (iii) to edit the completed schedules in some detail; and (iv) to undertake a dummy analysis on crucial parts of the schedule to see if the data that is wanted is really being obtained.

After all these points have been checked the schedule will be finally redrafted and the instructions also suitably amended. The schedule can then be printed or mimeographed and sent out in the hands of the interviewers whose major task has now begun. The core of this, as Moser says, "is to locate (or select) her sample members, to obtain interviews with them and to ask the questions and record the answers as instructed."[12]

Each interviewer will have been told to check that every blank is filled in with some appropriate symbol or response. As the completed schedules come in it will be necessary to see that they are all checked for accuracy by an editor and any queries answered immediately either by the interviewer herself or by her going back to inquire again.

In the course of drafting the schedule a good deal of attention must be paid to the form of the questions to see that they are clear and unambiguous. Responses must be examined to see that they are in fact yielding the required data. The example of the first mail questionnaire used by Kirk,[13] referred to in Chapter 4, may be instructive here. Kirk recounts how initially he had received little corroboration of a hypothesis that non-adopters frequently drew distinctions between adopted and non-adopted children, which were upsetting to the adopters. The question Kirk originally asked was "Has anyone ever made an unfriendly remark, or done something unpleasant or troublesome for you or your child, because they knew that the child is adopted?"[14] Only 15/97 said "yes". Kirk could well have taken these results at their face value and rejected his hypothesis. He would then have concluded that adopters were not treated differently from non-adopters because of the status of their children. He was suspicious of the replies because of the experience of his wife and himself as adoptive parents. He could clearly not generalize from his own case, especially in the face of the questionnaire responses. He could and did distrust whether his mail questionnaire had been sensitive enough an instrument to release the facts he wanted, in an area where both taboo and unpleasant emotion might operate. In the course of having a group of adoptive parents discuss the questionnaire in his presence, he noticed that this particular question was quickly passed over. Ultimately, by recounting his own and his wife's experiences, he was able to release similar accounts from other adoptive parents. As a result of this discussion Kirk, for his second mail questionnaire, replaced his simple questions by the much more sophisticated set of questions shown below:[15]

> Here is a list of some reactions which might at times be experienced by adoptive parents and children. For each kind of statement please check the appropriate columns to show whether something like this has been experienced in your family, and if it has happened, how frequently.

Type of Experience

a. An acquaintance remarks: "Isn't it wonderful of you to have taken this child!"

b. A woman says: "How lucky you are that you didn't have to go through all the trouble of pregnancy and birth like *I* had."

c. A friend asks: "Tell me, do you know anything about this child's background?"

d. A well-wisher says "He *is* a darling baby, and after all you can never know for sure how even your own will turn out."

e. Your child is asked by a playmate: "But who are your real parents?"

f. You are being introduced at a party and your host remarks: "They are those unselfish people with the adopted child."

g. A friend says: "This child looks so much like you he (she) could be your own."

h. Someone refers to your adopted child saying: "He (she) is certainly lucky to have you for parents."

i. A neighbour remarks: "How well you care for your child, just like a real mother."

j. You overhear someone saying: "Isn't it wonderful that he can be such a good father to a little boy who isn't his own son."

k. A visitor says: "It surely takes a special gift to love someone else's child like your own."

l. The mother of your child's playmate remarks: 'It's hard enough to know how to handle my Johnny when he's giving me trouble. I often wonder how you deal with the troublesome behaviour of a child who's adopted."

From this new set of questions Kirk was able to develop a refined hypothesis about the ways in which non-adoptive parents made it known to adopters that their families were "different". The response to his original, more naïve, question was some indication of the taboo surrounding the whole subject. The question itself assumed that adoptive parents would see this different view as a hostile one and would be able to acknowledge it as such.

Questions should be clear, unambiguous, and attempts should be made to see that they are measuring what they set out to measure. In addition at the drafting stage attention should be paid to the length of the questionnaire. A schedule for interviewing which is too long has two quite separate disadvantages: (i) that the respondents are so tired or irritated that towards the end they cease to be reliable in their replies, and (ii) that more data will be collected than can be analysed. The last point will be dealt with separately below.

On the first point great care must be taken. For most purposes, an optimum length for an interview is 20–30 minutes, but some may last an hour. A very great deal of information of a factual kind can be elicited in 10 minutes. How much data of other kinds can be collected in any given time depends a good deal on its nature. Some answers are near the surface of the respondents' minds, such as their age and how long they have been married, and what job they have. Other kinds of information require more thought. Most of us do not carry around in our heads a precise count of the number of people we have met in the last week, for example, or what the last quarter's fuel bill was. Yet these are matters of fact. Where feelings and attitudes are concerned they are likely to be harder to uncover, unless we are simply concerned with the stereotypes which lie near the surface. One of the objects of the pilot run on a new questionnaire should be to check it for length. It is never possible to collect all the information which it might be desirable to have, nor to put to all possible uses the information which has been collected. The best is to arrive at some sort of middle position, between what is desirable and what is manageable to collect and to analyse.

Certainly no unnecessary information should be collected. Interested parties may try to persuade you to add "just one more question". They should be resisted. Only collect the material that can be used and be clear from the beginning how you intend to use the material you do collect.

Since the object of most large-scale interviews is to discover the distribution of certain factors, or to discover whether two factors commonly go together, all the data collected must be submitted at some stage to a tabular form. Before the schedule of questions is drawn up a series of dummy tabulations, showing which data it is proposed to show against which, should be drawn up. It is not necessary actually to draw the blind tables, but to list what these are to show. Then the questions that it is proposed to ask can be tested against them. If there are questions which are not included in the proposed tabulations, one must ask whether an essential table is missing or whether the question is really unnecessary. Almost certainly in the end all the proposed tables will not prove fruitful and others, not anticipated, will be needed. The exercise of thinking through to the end of the proposed analysis, at the beginning of schedule construction, is a most salutory one. It is a reminder of the amount of work that is involved in analysis. The effort of collecting the data in the first place is often so great that many beginning research workers fail to realize that the analysis is likely to take much longer than the data collection took. It is possible that the increasing use of computers will alter this work schedule. On the other hand, it is probably more likely to make more extensive and sophisticated analysis possible. Thus at least in pieces of original work, more will be done rather than less time taken. In replicated studies undoubtedly the use of computers will speed up the exercise considerably. It is essential to understand the old methods of analysis, however, before proper use can be made of a computer. It is with this stage of learning in mind that this book is written. The methods of analysis are dealt with later in Chapter 8.

REFERENCES

1. BOSSARD, J. H. S., and BOLL, E. S., *The Large Family System*, Univ. of Pa. Press, 1956.
2. HYMAN, H. H., *et al.*, *Interviewing in Social Research*, Univ. of Chicago Press, 1955, is a comprehensive study.
3. MADGE, J., *The Tools of Social Science*, Longmans, 1965, p. 150.
4. GOODE, W. J., and HATT, P. K., *Methods in Social Research*, pp. 186 *et seq.*
5. MOSER, C. A., *Survey Methods in Social Investigation*, Heinemann, London, 1958, pp. 192 *et seq.* deals with selection and training of interviewers.
6. ROGERS, C. R., The non-directive method as a technique for social research, *Am. J. Sociol.* **50**, 279–83 (1945).
7 MERTON, R. K., and KENDALL, P. L., *The Focused Interview*, Free Press 1956.
8. GITTUS, E., Income in M. STACEY (Ed.), *Comparability of Data Collection and Presentation*, B.S.A. and S.S.R.C., Heinemann, 1969.
9. SELLTIZ, C., JAHODA, M., DEUTSCH, M., and COOK, S. W., *Research Methods in Social Relations*, Henry Holt, 1959, pp. 262 *et seq.*

10. Ibid.; Appendix C is an interesting discussion of questionnaire construction.

11. GOODE and HATT, *op cit.*, p. 195.

12. MOSER, *op. cit.*, p. 186, Chapters 11, 12, and 13 are useful and relevant to the present chapter.

13. KIRK, H. D., *Shared Fate: A Theory of Adoption and Mental Health*, Free Press of Glencoe, 1964.

14. *Ibid.*, p. 53.

15. *Ibid.*, pp. 28–29 and 175–6.

CHAPTER 6

Asking Questions: The Sample Survey

THE last chapter considered some of the problems involved in designing and asking questions. If the population to whom the questions are addressed is a large one, it will be necessary to ask the questions of a representative sample rather than of the entire population. In this case a sample survey is called for. Sometimes the information which is sought can be obtained more satisfactorily from key informants or from the detailed study of social groups, rather than from a sample of the general population.

Let us suppose that a town wishes to know whether it has an adequate provision of playing fields. The proportion of games players in the entire population is so small, perhaps only 10%, that to ask this question of a sample of the total population would be to ask at least nine ignorant persons for every one who might be helpful. In this case key informants, i.e. secretaries and committees of sports clubs, would produce much more information in much less time. It would clearly be important to make sure that all were covered, the well-provided and the ill-provided clubs alike. It would be important to be quite clear that each understood the same thing by "adequate". However, it may be objected that if the provision is markedly bad many potential games players will not have been enrolled and these could only be found through public inquiry. Furthermore, if the aim is not only to assess the adequacy of the provision, but also to discover how many players there are of certain games in a certain place, then a sample survey of the entire population may well be necessary.

A sample survey is the best way to find out information about a particular population either on a simple matter of fact, such as occupation, or religious or political allegiance. It may also be appropriate to a subject where the broad outlines have already been discovered by other means, and about which certain tentative hypotheses have already been formed, relating to particular social categories: rich, poor, widowed, single, male, female, etc. A survey may prove essential before any firm conclusions can be drawn from any piece of work, and generalizations made.

Given that it has been decided that a sample survey is needed, this chapter will outline the principle steps to be taken. It will not go into great detail about the statistical and allied problems involved. There are many excellent specialist books that do that.[1]

There are in principle two main methods of sampling: (i) *probability or random sampling* and (ii) *judgement sampling*.★ The feature which separates these two methods is that in the first case human judgement is in no way involved in the selection, whereas in the second case it enters at some stage of the proceedings. Random sampling should therefore not be confused with the haphazard selection of cases for study. When a man selects haphazardly he may think that his selection is not biased, but in fact his judgement has entered at each choice of case for study. There is no way of calculating what error may have entered the selection process. In the case of *random sampling* every unit in the population has a calculable and non-zero chance of selection. In *simple random sampling* every unit has an equal chance of selection. In some cases *stratified random sampling* is used. Before sampling the population is divided into a number of strata. Thus the student population in a particular university might be divided into first, second, and third years. Then within each strata a simple random sample is drawn. This will increase the precision of the sample if the basis of stratification is closely related to the subject of the survey. Thus if student opinion about careers is known to vary as their studies proceed, it might be reasonable to stratify by year in a study of this subject. This method can be particularly useful if the size of the strata vary considerably. A simple random sample might not in that case yield enough cases in the smaller groups. If one was concerned with sociology students,

★Throughout this section I shall use the terminology suggested by Moser.[1]

for example, it might be that all freshers took sociology in their first year, so that there was a large number in that year, but that in the second and third years students specialized, so that these strata contained far fewer students. The same argument can obviously be applied to social classes, but here there is the difficulty of not knowing in advance of survey how many there are in each class, and, also important, who is in each class. Samples can only be stratified in advance when the relevant factors are known. There are other systems of random sampling, e.g. cluster and multi-stage. Students are advised to consult the relevant textbooks for discussions of the use of these.[1] Whatever the method of sampling, so long as it is random, statistical theory can be applied and the limits of confidence that can be placed upon the sample can be calculated. That is to say it is possible to calculate the standard error of the sample and to say within what limits the sample is likely to be representative of the parent population from which it was drawn. There remain, of course, any errors which may have entered for other reasons. Non-response and errors in the source from which the sample was drawn being the major non-statistical sources.

Quota sampling is an often-used type of *judgemental sampling*. Whereas in random sampling the units for study, e.g. persons to be interviewed, are determined in advance, in the case of quota sampling the final selection is left to the interviewer. Certain quota controls will have been set in advance. That is, before the interviewer receives her instructions, it will have been determined that so many men and women, of given ages and social classes are to be interviewed. The interviewer will then be free to choose persons who fit these descriptions. Thus while the areas where the interviewers are to go may have been determined in advance by random methods, her judgement enters at the final stage, because she picks the respondents.

At the start of the sample survey it is important to be clear what is the population to be surveyed. The population may be defined by reference to a geographic area. This may be an administrative area, e.g. a parish, a municipal borough, a county borough, a nation state. Occasionally the social population neatly fits the administrative area. When the population does fit, many problems are automatically solved. Often, however, it does not. The residential area of a town which is to be studied may well spill over into the rural area round about. In this case a decision must be reached as to whether the "town" for the purposes of the research is to be the administrative area, which will do violence to the social facts and exclude some people who could call themselves members of the town, or whether a more realistic social area is to be taken and the newer dormitory areas to be included. In this case, difficulties will inevitably be involved in sampling and in comparison of the collected data with official records. Much will depend on the subject of the research which course is taken and each research worker must decide for himself which are the lesser disadvantages. This he can do if he understands the problems in principle. What is the ideal area depends on the subject of his research. It may be that ideally he wants to study the town dwellers, including those who live in the surrounding area still administered by the rural authority. If he decides to do this how can he sample them and with what can he compare his results?

In order to obtain a random sample of any population it is necessary to have available a complete list of all the population concerned. Thus, in the case of a university, it is presumed the registry will have a complete list of all staff and students. In the case of a factory a list of the complete pay roll is in existence. In the case of a town the most common place to find a list of the majority of adult inhabitants is the electoral register. Most people living in that place on the 1st of October, and over 21 years of age, are entitled to a vote and should therefore be listed by name.* The electoral register is public property being open to inspection and available for purchase from the offices of the local returning officer. So long as it is not required to sample the total population of the town, including the most recent arrivals and the children and young people under 21, this is, for Britain, a good basis for sampling. (The document from which a sample is drawn is called a *sampling frame*.) It is possible to sample the adult population within any major

*Certain persons, e.g. aliens, are excluded.

administrative area. From this one may reasonably, within statistical limits, infer certain things about the adult population of that administrative area. It is also the area for which certain official records are kept. Since these are kept for government purposes they relate to administrative areas. This can be most helpful in many kinds of research. The official data can provide a check upon the validity of the sample and the sample data can be related to official findings in other ways.

The town to be studied may be a borough plus part of the surrounding rural area. In this case what one does in deciding upon the population to be defined depends entirely upon the research. If the important factor in the research is the town as a functioning unit for social and economic purposes, then it may be necessary to sacrifice the advantages of comparability and administrative neatness, despite the sampling and validation problems which are created. If, however, the dominant concern is with the town as an administrative unit, or comparability of the research data with administrative data, then it may be worth while to substitute administrative neatness for social reality. In some circumstances it may be essential to effect a compromise.

This is the situation which has occurred in Banbury between the two studies.* Around 1950, with the exception of one neighbouring village which was rapidly becoming a dormitory area, the whole of the town was defined by the borough boundary and physically distinguished from the surrounding administrative rural districts by a belt of farm land. This belt was partly in the borough and partly in the rural districts. The administrative boundary of the municipal borough coincided with other definitions of the town. It is true that persons from surrounding villages came to work in the borough. But for the most part it could reasonably be said that these were village people coming to town to work. In 1966, as we approach once more the matter of drawing a sample of the Banbury population, we find that Banbury cannot be defined as it was in 1950. The built-up area of the town joins with the built-up area of the villages

*The Nuffield Foundation, which grant-aided the first Banbury study,[2] made a grant for a second study in 1966.

in a number of places. The village that was just becoming a dormitory suburb in 1950 is now entirely such. Others are following. For some purposes Banbury can no longer be defined as co-extensive with the municipal borough. Thus when the town is again studied the sample will be drawn, not only from the electoral registers of the municipal borough, but from some of those which relate to the surrounding rural districts. At the same time it will be necessary to compare the information collected for the town with information collected for administrative reasons and with the information collected in 1950 for the first survey. Thus the data will have to be collected in such a way that it can be tabulated to show (a) the administrative area, (b) the surrounding rural districts, and (c) the two parts added together. This is quite possible, but a nuisance because it involves three lots of tabulation where one previously was enough. Nevertheless, this seems to be a circumstance in which the requirements of the research cannot be met except by going to this extra trouble and expense. The requirements being that (a) the present town of Banbury is studied, and (b) that it is studied in such a way as to make comparison with the previous study possible. The town of Banbury today is not defined by its borough boundaries as clearly as it was in 1950. Thus no short cut is possible.

In some kinds of research the population to be studied is not only defined territorially but also by some other characteristic, indeed another characteristic may be dominant. Thus one may be interested in studying all persons who have been discharged from a particular hospital in the past year, for example, and who live in a particular place; or one may be interested in all those who have been discharged from the hospital in the past year regardless of where they live. In this last case the sampling frame will have nothing at all to do with locality, but will be the register kept in the hospital, which records all such discharges and the date at which they took place. Fortunately, hospitals tend to be reasonably well-organized bureaucracies from this point of view and keep such registers. Permission to have access to the register for sampling purposes may be harder to come by. Seeking such permissions is an inevitable part of research work which is often a good deal more time consuming than expected.

In cases where a sampling frame, such as the electoral register, or a list of hospital discharges is concerned, the sample can only be as good as the frame from which it was drawn. There will inevitably be statistical errors in the sample. These fortunately, in a random sample, can be measured.[3] The errors which exist in the frame itself and which are inevitably mirrored in the sample drawn, cannot be measured. It may be that their nature, where they exist, can be assessed and it is important that this should be done wherever possible, so that some idea is gained of which way the bias may run. Thus we know that an electoral register tends to be out of date before it is operative because of deaths and removals, even if the inclusion of young (Y) voters reduces the error at the other end caused by those who have come of age since it was drawn up. The errors due to removals are likely to be of different kinds in different areas, depending on what sections of the population are removing and for what reasons. These errors can rarely be measured with any precision.

Sometimes it may be necessary to use, as a sampling frame, records which have no pretension to be very precise. Thus to sample the child population, for some information connected with health, it may be necessary to use health visitors' lists. Such lists tend to include people who have newly moved to the area, as the visitors are notified of them or come across them in the course of their rounds and tend therefore to be reasonably inclusive, but the lists may well also include a number of cases who have moved away and whose records have not yet been sent on. Such an administrative time lag is almost inevitable in a free country where people can come and go at will. Thus the sampling frame here is likely to include a number of non-existent persons. This is also likely to be the case in sampling from a local authority's housing waiting list. This will include all people actively seeking a council house, but also will include a number who were in this position a few years ago, who have now moved out of the area, or acquired a house privately and who have failed to notify the local authority of their changed position. On the other hand, immediately after a waiting list review has taken place, the error may run the other way. The usual review procedure is that applicants who wish to keep their names on the list should notify the authority. Some who do wish their names to remain on the list will fail to inform the authority or some other human error will intervene. At this stage, therefore, the list will not contain "dead" applicants but may well also not contain persons who *are* actively seeking a house. None of these omissions would matter if they were randomly distributed throughout the waiting-list population. The likelihood is that they are not. People who have one factor in common may well have other factors also in common. These factors may even relate to the subject of the inquiry. Those who fail to write in may be the most busy or the least literate, for example.

None of these problems are entirely soluble. Sometimes partial solutions can be found. What is important is that no research worker should be deluded into thinking that a neatly typed list, because it looks official, is necessarily a perfect reflection of the social reality. It is part of the research worker's job to find out where it may deviate from the reality. In the majority of cases public servants are well aware of the limitations of the administrative instruments with which they work and are willing and pleased to explain these.

Occasionally it is impossible for the area, or the type of person with whom one is concerned, to find a suitable frame. Thus, while it may be easy, given official permission, to obtain from an educational authority a list of all school children in that authority's schools, this is quite different from getting a list of all school children living in that authority's area. Some will go to private schools in the area. Others may go to schools outside the area. The importance of a *clear definition of the population in question* is plain.

Where there is no clear frame from which to sample, other expedients must be resorted to which will be considered under the heading of drawing a sample. In general the research worker decides (i) how to define the population to be sampled, and (ii) how to obtain a sampling frame which lists the population. Then he goes on to the next move which is (iii) to draw the sample.

To do this he must first decide whether to use a random or a quota sample. Statisticians tend always to favour some method of random sampling because the standard error of the sample is measurable, and to criticize quota sampling for its theoretical weakness, while, as Moser says, "market and opinion researchers have defended quota sampling for its cheapness and administrative convenience".[4] For most research purposes a random sample is to be preferred if it is obtainable, i.e. if there is a reliable sampling frame available.

Let us suppose that it has been decided to sample a population using the electoral register. The next decision must be the size of the sample that is to be drawn. This must be looked at both in terms of the absolute size of the sample itself, and in terms of the sample as a proportion of the parent population, i.e. the *sampling fraction*. Detailed discussions of sample size can be found in any statistics textbook.[5] In general, a sample must be large enough for any breakdown in analysis to leave one with meaningful numbers. Thus the larger the parent population and the fewer the subdivisions needed in the final analysis, the smaller the sampling fraction can be. On the other hand if multiple subdivisions are needed in analysis, or the attributes of small sections of the population are of interest, it is advisable to take a larger fraction. In any case, when thinking of sample size, it should be noted as a rough guide that samples of less than fifty present special problems. It is also important to note that the accuracy of a particular statistic derived from a sample survey, i.e. the size of the sampling error, depends on the size of the sample and *not* the size of the total population or the sampling fraction. The population size will only enter into the estimate of the standard error when the sampling fraction is high, say 10% or more. Thus a sample of 2000 persons is usually adequate for simple analysis of data in a national survey, but a sample of the *same size* would be needed for a similar degree of accuracy in a local survey.

Let us suppose that it has been decided to draw a 5% sample to yield 2000 names from the electoral registers of three adjacent parliamentary divisions. Ideally, each person should be given a number and the names selected either by the use of tables of random numbers,[6] or by putting slips with all the numbers in a hat and drawing out the requisite quantity. Often a method known as *quasi-random* sampling, or *systematic sampling from lists*, is used. In this method every, say, twentieth name starting from a point randomly determined is marked on the list. This is systematic and thus ensures that no human bias enters into the selection. It is possible, however, that the list is compiled in such an order that persons with certain attributes are not distributed randomly throughout the list.

As indicated earlier, to permit detailed analysis of groups which are a small section of the population, it may be possible to stratify the sample and make the random selection within the strata. This would avoid a large increase in sample size. Suppose one wished to examine the attributes of, say, large-income earners in a factory, compared with other earners. Large-income earners are likely to constitute only a small proportion of the pay roll. To achieve enough large-income earners from a simple random sample might require so large a sample as to be prohibitive. The procedure would be to group the income earners on the factory pay roll into, say, those with small, medium, and large incomes on some agreed dividing lines. Having done this a different sampling fraction could be fixed for each of the three groups, one which would yield, say, 200 cases in each group. Thus a 5% sample of the low income earners might be enough, while a 10% sample of the middle group might be needed and perhaps as much as 20% in the large income group. The sample would then be drawn according to the fraction determined in each of the groups separately. If we imagine that the earners in each of the three income groups are recorded on index cards in each of three filing drawers, one could then select every twentieth card in the low income drawer; every tenth card in the medium income drawer, and every fifth card in the large income drawer, giving 200 names in each case. This procedure can only be used when the distribution of the attribute in question (in this case income) is known in advance, as in this case it is from the payroll.

There are other ways in which samples can be stratified. It is sometimes done by region, for example, or urban or rural areas in the case of national sample. Once again any standard textbook will explain the procedures involved.[7]

Sometimes it is essential to sample a population for which no sampling frame is available. This is regrettable and to be avoided wherever possible, but sometimes is quite unavoidable.

Two solutions are possible. One is to use a quota sample, which has the advantages and disadvantages already discussed. The other is more expensive and time-consuming. It involves taking a rapid census of the population and sampling from the lists specially prepared for the purpose. If inadequate data is available from which quota controls can be prepared the last alternative must be pursued.

Collecting the data. When the sample is decided upon and the pilot completed the interviewing team can go out into the field, find their respondents, fill in their schedules of questions, and bring them back into the office for editing and checking. In a large-scale study it may well be necessary to have a percentage of the inquiries checked up on by sending someone on a repeat call. It has been known for interviewers on a wet day to conduct an imaginary interview with a distant respondent while sitting comfortably at home. It has also been known for interviewers to interview wives and record for husbands. Some check on such human failings is necessary and these checks must be formalized in large samples. It is also necessary that the editing of the schedule for errors and omissions should be done as quickly as possible. It may be merely a failure to record on the interviewer's part. She may know the answer. On the other hand, she may have forgotten to put the question, in which case she will have to go back and ask again. In the course of editing it is important to note contradictory information. Depending on the purpose of the survey it may or may not be necessary to get this cleared up with the respondent. Sometimes the very inconsistencies are what give a clue to a situation. People can, for example, hold contradictory opinions which they apply at different times and circumstances. It may be helpful to know this.

Once as many questionnaires have been completed as seems possible one is almost ready to proceed to the analysis. Before this it is just necessary to see how the sample that has been completed compares with the sample that was drawn, that is to determine the *non-response rate*. For the list of completed questionnaires will not be quite the same as the sample list. There will have been errors in the sampling list. Some people whose names were drawn will have gone away or died. Others will have refused to reply. How many will refuse depends a good deal on the nature of the inquiry. It is sometimes said that there are 4% of door slammers anyway, people who just do not care to co-operate in matters of this kind. Sometimes, however, 100% response is gained from those who are actually contacted. This has happened in inquiries about children's health for example. Other inquiries on matters that involve very personal or private matters may expect a higher refusal rate. Those which ask a good deal of the respondent may also expect this. Thus the *Family Expenditure Survey*[8] of the Ministry of Labour has quite a low response rate, 71–74% of the effective sample (1960–2). This is partly because many people think that money matters are their private affair, and partly because keeping the accounts of day-by-day expenditure, which is required by the survey, is an exacting business and many people cannot be bothered to do it.

In addition to those who have moved or died, and those who refuse, there will be another category who cannot be found. There must be considerable care taken about these non-contacts. Interviewing for a sample survey is not a job with comfortable set hours. Suppose it is a sample of women; suppose all the interviews are done between 9 a.m. and 5 p.m.; there will be a considerable non-response rate. This might not matter if one could assume that it was evenly scattered throughout the female population. Almost certainly it will not be. The interviewers will have caught all those women who do not go out to employed work in the day and will have missed all those who do. Those who go out to work are likely to be different from those who stay at home in lots of ways connected with their working. They are likely to be younger on the one hand and more-middle-aged on the other, than those who stay at home. The ones at home are likely to include a high proportion of mothers of young children and also of women past retiring age. The home-bound women certainly are in no way representative of all women. Thus interviewers will have been told that they must call back, perhaps three times, and these "call-backs" must be made at different times

of the day, and may have to be at the weekend. Despite all these efforts there will be a proportion of non-contacts. Thus when all the questionnaires are in, a table must be drawn up showing the number sampled; the number completed; the number refused; the number that cannot be traced (removed, house empty, not known etc.); and the number that could not be contacted for other reasons. It is advisable to tabulate any information that may be available about the refusals and non-contacts of all kinds to see if they bunch about a particular characteristic at all. Thus in Britain the rateable value of the house is available at the offices of the rating authority.*
There is a known tendency for persons in more highly rated houses to refuse more often than others; this can be checked. Refusals are likely also to be persons of higher income, higher occupation status, and higher educational attainment than average. This may well be relevant to the subject of the inquiry in one way or another. If the sample is of all adult men and women, some idea of the proportions of the sexes to be expected can be gained from the electoral register, if this was the sampling frame, and possibly also from the census if data for the relevant area is available. How useful a check such as the census is depends on how long ago the census was taken in the area concerned. What checks can be found will depend on the sampling frame, the subject of the inquiry and the area. Wherever possible some check should be found. Sometimes no check is possible. In this case reliance must simply be placed on the care taken in planning and executing the work. Furthermore, because the checks come out right, for example there are 50 men to every 50 women which is what you would expect from other sources for the population in hand, it does not follow that some other error, unconnected with sex, has not crept in, an error upon which you may have no check at all. Thus there might have been a bias in the non-contact rate towards single persons in their early twenties. This might have affected males and females equally for the reason that the unmarried in this age group come home from work, take their tea, and are off out again courting (this affecting both

*County boroughs, municipal boroughs and urban and rural districts are rating authorities in England and Wales.

sexes equally) as soon as they have finished. In this case they would be difficult to catch at home.* A sex break-down would not show this. An age break-down against which to check would show it, but there is not always an age break-down to hand. Clearly mal-representation in an unmeasured factor can always happen. It is encouraging if the factors that can be checked come out right, but does not mean that no biases have entered. A good slice of common sense and listening to what the interviewers have to say about their experiences is important in running to earth any hidden errors there may be.

Now all the questionnaires are in and checked and the surveyors have a good idea just how much reliance they may place on the data and how to measure its deficiencies. They are now ready to proceed to the stage of analysis.

REFERENCES

1. MOSER, C. A., *Survey Methods in Social Investigation*, Heineman, London, 1958, is the obvious British work.
   KISH, L., *Survey Sampling*, Wiley, 1965, is a major recent American study covering the whole field of survey sampling.
   CONNOLLY, T. G., and SLUCKIN, W., *An Introduction to Statistics for the Social Sciences*, London, Cleaver Hume, 1958; chaps. VI and VII deal with the statistical aspects of sampling in an introductory manner.
2. STACEY, M., *Tradition and Change: A Study of Banbury*, O.U.P., 1960.
3. CONNOLLY and SLUCKIN, *op. cit.*, chap. VI.
   MOSER, *op cit.*, chap. V.
   KISH, *op. cit.*, *passim*.
4. MOSER, *op. cit.*, esp. chap. VI.
   KISH, *op. cit.*, *passim*.
5. MOSER, *op. cit.*, chap. VII.
   KISH, *op. cit.*, *passim*.
6. MOSER, *op. cit.*, pp. 119 ff.
7. MOSER, *op. cit.*, chap. VI.
   KISH, *op. cit.*, esp. chap. 3.
8. MINISTRY OF LABOUR, *Family Expenditure Survey: Report for 1962*, London, H.M.S.O. 1963.

---

*In actual fact, in the cultures I have dealt with, the young men have usually been a good deal harder to catch at home than the young women.

CHAPTER 7

Combined Operations

USING SEVERAL METHODS FOR ONE STUDY

It will have become obvious to the reader by now that for most
sorts of social research except a matter of counting simple facts
about certain social categories, more than one method must be used.
The various methods that can be used in the exploratory stage were
explained in Chapter 3 and included examination of documents, of
statistical records, and the interview of key informants. For some
kinds of research secondary analyses may be the main method
of the research. In Chapter 4 it was suggested that observations,
whether participant or not, need to be checked by more wide-
ranging surveys. On the other hand, questionnaire techniques can
only be used satisfactorily in a subject where a good deal is already
known. Since the number of questions which can be selected is
limited, and their form fixed in many cases, it is important that the
key questions should be asked in such a way that a reliable response
will be elicited. This is particularly difficult, as the case of Kirk shows,
where the question is one near to a taboo subject or involving a good
deal of emotion.

It may be helpful to recall some pieces of research which have
used a variety of methods. Bossard and Boll found that in an
exploratory study of the large family system it was useful to use the
personal document and the personal interview.[1] In the first
instance they wrote to their respondents and asked them to write an
account of their experiences as members of large families. Some
wrote at length, others briefly. Wherever possible the same respondents were interviewed. In all cases one method was a check on the
other. In some, brief documents were greatly amplified by face-to-

face discussion. In others, the document was more revealing than the interview.

In a quite different study, that of Banbury,[2] a number of methods were used. The research problem, the consequences of immigration in a market town, was itself defined in the course of initial participant observation. This method continued throughout, bias being avoided, as Chapter 4 showed, by the use of three research workers who checked on each other's reports and assessments. Nevertheless, some of the data collected through participant observation or through direct observation cannot be properly assessed without other facts to set it against. Until we knew how many of the people living in Banbury in 1950 were immigrants we had no facts by which to assess the meaning of the oft-repeated comments about the town being flooded by immigrants, about how you used to know everybody and now you hardly knew anybody. A sample survey showed that the residents were about half and half, Banburian and immigrant. This meant, looked at from the Banburian point of view, for every one of "us" (natives) there was now one of "them" (immigrants). From the Banburians' statements one might have expected that there were now more immigrants than Banburians, that the latter were outnumbered. This was not so as the sample survey showed. Thus it was clear that the statements meant something more than could be explained by the numbers of immigrants alone: they were descriptions of the changes which had been seen to come concurrently with the immigrants rather than comments on the numbers of immigrants.*

The information collected in the course of participant observation is revealing, especially to the observer. It is hard to transmit to others, except in a wordy and descriptive manner, and even more difficult to prove the truth of the insights received. More systematic observation can sometimes turn such insights, or field work hunches, into demonstrable facts.

Thus we had the strong impression from participant observation that there were groups in Banbury which overlapped each other making some kind of larger and looser group, that some cliques we

*Also they revealed attitudes to immigrants.

met were parts, somehow, of a larger whole. This impression was gained from the sharing and shifting of members between and among groups; from the hints gained in conversation about "who knew whom". We also had the impression that there were other cliques and groups, similarly overlapping among themselves as if they might also be part of a larger whole. We saw no overlapping between the two sets, however, and thought that the larger wholes must be two separate groupings. In a small village we could have checked on this through continued and extensive participant observation, for in a village of 200 or 300 we could have moved among the people enough to find out whether the first set of cliques overlapped anywhere with the second. In a town the size of Banbury (then about 19,000 population) this was not possible. Because we *saw* no overlapping between all the cliques we could not assume that such overlapping did not take place. It might have occurred in one of the pubs which it was not possible for us to be in (even three young and strong research workers cannot cover sixty-odd pubs in one evening). Some other method of checking was necessary.

We therefore used the method of analysing the leadership of voluntary associations as a check on groupings. As the book describes, we listed all voluntary associations. We then interviewed the secretary or another officer of each and obtained certain facts from him about the association's history and activities and about its committee members. This was an interview of key informants using a partly structured focused technique. The key informants were defined by their office in a voluntary association. Certain closed questions were asked of them all: name, number, age group, sex, and occupation, of all their executive committee members. These included no questions which were not common knowledge. Other, open-ended questions were asked of them all, about the history of the association, for example. The method of analysis of the data about committee members was important. We were interested in larger social groupings within the town and if there proved to be a number of groups which had no connection at all with another lot, as we suspected, we were interested in where these breaks came. We therefore put the associations which were mutually exclusive as far from each other as possible on a large sheet of paper. Thus we set apart the major denominations (since most people only espouse one faith at a time) and the three political parties (again one usually only has one political allegiance at a time). With the frame this gave us we then added all the voluntary associations drawing one line linking two associations for every person who was a committee member of each. This showed that some associations clustered together and that between these clusters there were breaks. In this way we were able to confirm, what we had suspected from participant observation, that above the level of face-to-face groupings there were larger groupings of which the face-to-face groups were a part. Also we could see that these larger groupings were to a considerable extent distinct and separate within the town. Overlapping had not been taking place behind our backs as we quite properly had suspected it might. We had tried and failed to falsify our hypotheses and we now had a much clearer idea of what these larger groupings were and how they were composed. On the other hand, from the study of overlapping committee membership on its own, we could not have inferred as much or indeed anything about the structure of groups in the town. On its own it would simply have been a study of the overlapping between committee members in a particular town. One could not have said what relation this bore to the total social structure. Without participant observation as well one would have had no idea whether people who were not connected in voluntary activities were not connected informally. When the gaps in social relations which were observed informally were seen to coincide broadly with those gaps revealed by the overlapping committee members method, it became more permissible to draw tentative conclusions about the broader social structure.

There still remained limits to understanding and to permissible inference. The leaders (defined as executive committee members) of formal associations, indeed the members themselves, might not be at all representative of the total population. Indeed, we knew from participant observation that this was so. We knew that middle-class people seemed to belong to a wider range of associations than working-class people. How much of the town did the association's leaders represent? Where did they fit in? A schedule inquiry of 20% of the population provided certain facts about it. The distribution of occupational status, of the leaders compared with the rank and file and with the town as a whole, showed that the leaders tended to be drawn from higher occupational status groups than the rank and file. Indeed, leaders and members tended as a whole to be drawn disproportionately from those with a higher status.

Thus to gain a picture of the total social scene and of the relations of the parts of the structure to the whole, many small face-to-face groups were studied by participant observation. Interviews with key informants yielded data on a number of different aspects of the life of the town, and a schedule inquiry into a 20% sample of the total population provided data about the major social categories within which the observed social groups fell.

The study into the hospitalization of young children which at the time of writing is in hand at Swansea University College also combines two sociological techniques, as Chapter 4 showed. The first was a diary record by the observer stressing particularly interaction. The second was a method of observation of the frequency of interaction controlled by a predetermined schedule and time-sampling. The two methods complement each other, the first having a quality of depth and the second of precision, which the other lacks.

INTER-DISCIPLINARY STUDY

The same study illustrates another aspect of the combined operation in research. That is when two or more disciplines are concerned in one study. The object of the Swansea hospital study is to observe the child as he moves from the home-centred social system to the hospital system and back again. This problem involves not only sociology but psychology, for in moving from the home-centred to the hospital system the child is subjected to two socialization processes—the home-centred and the hospital ones. This is likely to affect his personality structure. How and in what way is a psychological problem. Therefore the same children who are being followed in their movements by a sociologist are also being followed by a psychiatrist. The psychiatrist using a doll play projection technique[3] and recording the child's reactions on each occasion examines him before, and three times after, hospitalization, the last occasion being 6 months after discharge. The object is not only to have two studies, one sociological and one psychiatric, but also to show the interrelations between the social systems involved and the personalities of the children. Thus one hopes to show an interrelation between social relations in the ward and subsequent personality as tested. In this research the two disciplines are very closely dependent on each other and working on the same few cases.

In some other kinds of research the dependence is no less great but of a different order. The Lower Swansea Valley Project[4] may be cited as an example here. The Lower Swansea Valley is an area of industrial dereliction presenting problems of rehabilitation concerned particularly with the difficulties of restoring plant life, of building on tip land, of restoration of social and economic life. It is a special problem in urban renewal and as with so many applied problems required a multi-disciplinary approach. Therefore six university departments of Swansea University College were involved in research, before a plan suggesting how the area might be restored could be evolved. The Botany Department was concerned with the restoration of plant life; the Geography Department with the mapping of the tip lands; the Geology Department with determining the rock structure of the valley; the Civil Engineering Department with the soil mechanics of the tipped valley floor; the Economics Department with the industrial prospects of the valley as part of a sub-region; while the sociologist was concerned with the human ecology of the area and its future in relation to housing and open space.

Each of these departments pursued its own researches, but each was kept fully informed of the other's progress, for no final recommendations for land use could have been made without cognizance being taken of all aspects. While it is probably fairer to describe the study as multi-disciplinary than inter-disciplinary, it is true to say that beyond the basic research within each discipline further relevant researches could not be made without absorbing the results of the researches of other disciplines.

In conclusion, combined operations are frequently needed in social research. These are of two principal kinds:

(1) The use of several methods within one research project to collect and check the data and to test an hypothesis.
(2) The collaboration more or less closely with other disciplines when a research subject falls on the frontiers of disciplines. This may be especially necessary in applied research, when the factors known from the other disciplines cannot be held constant.[5]

REFERENCES

1. BOSSARD, J. H. S., and BOLL, E. S., *The Large Family System*, Univ. of Pa. Press, 1956.
2. STACEY, M., *Tradition and Change: A Study of Banbury*, O.U.P., 1960.
3. The London Doll Play Technique designed by Terence Moore, see T. MOORE, *J. Child Psychol. Psychiat.* 5, 1964.
4. HILTON, K. J. (Ed.) *The Lower Swansea Valley Project*, Longmans, London, 1967.
5. GLUCKMAN, M., *Closed Systems and Open Minds. The Limits of Naivety in Social Anthropology*, Oliver and Boyd, 1964.

CHAPTER 8

Analysing the Data

OFTEN the effort of collecting the data is so considerable that, having finished and gathered it all in, the researcher feels that the job must be almost done. This is far from the case. He has now many interesting, but unreliable, impressions and a mass of data which, as they stand, are meaningless. The data were collected on the assumption that they would demonstrate certain patterns of human behaviour and now they must be sorted out to see if they do yield any patterns and if these are the expected patterns. By now what the researcher expects is likely to be his original hypotheses modified by his subsequent impressions. As has been said before, the analysis is likely to take much longer than the data collection took.

There are many forms of analysis that can be used. Which ones are relevant depends partly on the kind of data and partly on what is wanted out of it. Data about kin, about friendship cliques, about social interaction in factory, hospital ward, or street will call for a quite different kind of analysis from the data collected in a random sample survey.[1] Since in Chapter 7 we left random sample surveys at the point where a survey was ready for analysis, let us start there. Within this broad group there are many kinds of analysis possible.

Let us suppose that we are simply interested in forecasting the result of the election, that people have been asked whether they will vote for Party A, Party B, or Party C. Some will have indicated a party and others will have said they "don't know", are undecided, or that they "don't vote." The replies may simply be sorted into four piles A, B, C, and don't know, don't vote, etc. It may be that the differences between piles A, B, and C, taking into account the sampling error (see Chapter 7) are so small that if the persons in pile 4 decided to vote in a particular way their actions could alter our predictions. Therefore we might want to know a good deal more about them, perhaps to separate the "undecided" and "don't know" from the "never vote" and "don't vote" replies. If this category was still so large that it was bigger than the difference between A and B, B and C, or C and A, we would be able to say only that the issue was in doubt, depending on the behaviour of the "don't knows". It might be, however, that this category was so small that it would not affect the issue. A prediction would then be more possible.

If we had collected people's voting intentions simply to predict the result of a particular election, our job would be finished. If, however, our interest in voting behaviour was not simply, or not at all, to predict election results, but because we were interested in other things about voters, or about voters as indicative of some characteristics of the social structure, our job would only just have begun. In Banbury interest was centred in the interrelations between institutions, and the voting behaviour of the population was interesting in so far as it could be shown to relate to other aspects of the social structure. One example of this concern was the interrelationship between social class and political allegiance. Income and occupation were taken as indicators of social class and the data was reproduced in Table 11 of *Tradition and Change*. A relationship was assumed to exist between class and voting behaviour and the nature of this relationship was examined.

That table indicated quite clearly that it was dealing only with the sample population about whom income, occupation, and voting behaviour were known. By implication the table made plain the number of persons for whom these data were unknown. However, the distribution of this category was not shown. Tables 1 and 2 have therefore been extracted from the original data and show not only income and occupation by voting, but also the distribution of the unknowns. Table 1 shows that of those who refused to state their income, a half were Conservative voters, another quarter being those who refused to state not only their income but also their politics. It is clear also from this table that since the size of the

TABLE 1. VOTING AND INCOME

Voting		−£249		£250–£499		£500+		Refused, etc.		Total	
		No.	%	No.	%	No.	%	No.	%	No.	%
Conservative	No.	205	35·7	221	28·3	40	51·9	58	50·4	524	33·8
	%		39·1		42·2		7·6		11·1		100·0
Labour	No.	190	33·0	364	46·5	15	19·5	13	11·3	582	37·6
	%		32·6		62·5		2·6		2·2		99·9
Liberal	No.	49	8·5	41	5·2	6	7·8	8	7·0	104	6·7
	%		47·1		39·4		5·8		7·7		100·0
Floaters and others	No.	16 }	2·8	20 }	2·6	3 }	3·9	2 }	1·7	41 }	2·6
	%	} 58		} 54		} 8		} 7		} 127	
		} 45·7		} 42·5		} 6·3		} 5·5		} 100·0	
None	No.	42 }	7·3	34 }	4·3	5 }	6·5	5 }	4·3	86 }	5·6
	%										
Refused and Don't Know	No.	73	12·7	102	13·0	8	10·4	29	25·2	212	13·6
	%		34·4		48·1		3·8		13·7		100·0
TOTAL	No.	575	100·0	782	99·9	77	100·0	115	99·9	1549	99·9
	%		37·1		50·5		5·0		7·4		100·0

ANALYSING THE DATA   111

TABLE 2. VOTING AND OCCUPATIONAL STATUS

Voting		1 and 2		3 and 4		5		6		7		R. and D.K.		Total	
		No.	%	No.	%	No.	%	No.	%	No.	%	No.	%	No.	%
Conservative	No.	35	57·4	139	50·5	163	29·4	70	21·1	27	15·9	18	25·0	452	30·9
	%	7·7		30·7		36·1		15·5		6·0		4·0		100·0	
Labour	No.	5	8·2	50	18·2	231	41·7	182	55·0	94	55·3	9	12·5	571	39·0
	%	0·9		8·75		40·45		31·9		16·5		1·6		100·0	
Liberal	No.	3	4·9	28	10·2	35	6·3	7	2·1	7	4·1	3	4·2	83	5·7
	%	3·6		33·7		42·2		8·4		8·4		3·6		99·9	
Floaters and others	No.	4 ⎱ 6·6		5 ⎱ 1·8		15 ⎱ 2·7		6 ⎱ 1·8		5 ⎱ 2·9		2 ⎱ 2·8		37 ⎱ 2·5	
	{combined}	7		17		38		22		16		4		104	
	%	6·7		16·3		36·5		21·2		15·4		3·8		99·9	
None	No.	3 ⎰ 4·9		12 ⎰ 4·4		23 ⎰ 4·2		16 ⎰ 4·8		11 ⎰ 6·5		2 ⎰ 2·8		67 ⎰ 4·6	
Refused and Don't Know	No.	11	18·0	41	14·9	87	15·7	50	15·1	26	15·3	38	52·8	253	17·3
	%	4·3		16·2		34·4		19·8		10·3		15·0		100·0	
TOTAL	No.	61	100·0	275	100·0	554	100·0	331	99·9	170	100·0	72	100·1	1463	100·0
	%	4·2		18·8		37·8		22·6		11·6		4·9		99·9	

"refused, etc." category of income is so large compared with the category £500+, its distribution among the three categories of income used could materially affect the relative proportions in each of these categories. Although these distributions were not shown in the original table, account was, of course, taken of them in the analysis. They were thought to be unlikely in the circumstances to affect the conclusions drawn. It could be argued, however, that if all the Conservatives who refused their incomes happened to fall in the lowest income group the picture would be very considerably altered: 41·5% of all those with incomes under £249 p.a. after tax would now be Conservative voters and nearly 47% of Conservative voters would fall in the lowest income bracket. If they all fell in the highest income group the number of persons in receipt of large incomes and voting Conservative would be doubled. Other evidence suggests that the association between high income, high occupational status, and non-Labour voting is probably in the direction indicated by the figures displayed which are based on responses received.[2] The refusals probably weakened the association which is indicated, Conservative-voting high-income receivers having a tendency to refuse to answer questions of this kind.

The general tendency, which was displayed in Table 11 in *Tradition and Change*, made it possible to make the following statements:

> The principal difference between supporters of the Labour and Con-
> servative parties . . . lies along social class lines. Almost all members of
> the middle class are Conservative . . . and almost all supporters of the
> Labour Party are working class. . . . Over 60% of all non-manual occu-
> pational classes (Hall/Jones scale) are Conservative voters, while only 20%
> are Labour voters. . . . Fifty-eight per cent of all manual classes vote
> Labour, but the working class nature of Labour Party support is most
> clearly indicated by the fact that 90% of Labour voters are in manual
> classes (Hall/Jones scale 5–7). Similarly, while 58% of those earning
> £500 p.a. or more after tax are Conservative, and of those earning under
> £500, 48% are Labour voters, 97% of all Labour voters earn under £500
> per annum.[3]

This example shows the importance of looking at the proportions of the distribution across the tabulation, as well as down. For this reason Tables 1 and 2 have been set out as one might set them out for analysis, not as one would present them for publication, i.e. they show in one table the percentages across and down. Propositions about the income and occupational characteristics of Conservative voters can only be determined by reading across and making statements about the proportion of the total Conservative voters in each income or occupation category. Statements about the behaviour of low-income earners, or persons in low-status occupations, can only be made by looking at the total distribution of voting behaviour among the total of such low-income or low-status categories (i.e. reading down). It is only out of the combination of these two ways of looking at the tabulation that one can reach the statement that the majority of high-income receivers are Conservative, or at least not Labour, but the majority of Labour voters are low-income receivers (taking £550 as the divide between "high" and "low" for these purposes). The statement that those of non-manual occupational status (categories 1, 2, 3, and 4) tend to vote Conservative while the majority of Labour voters are manual workers (categories 5, 6, and 7) is similarly derived. In so far as occupation and income may be taken as indicators of class, one may conclude from this that middle-class people tend to vote Conservative, but Labour voters are nearly all working class. This is not the same thing as saying that working-class people tend to vote Labour. An inspection of the Table, for example, shows that over one-third of the lowest income groups voted Conservative. This can be stated, perhaps, as the proposition that "there is a tendency for non-manual workers to vote Conservative which is stronger and more consistent than the tendency of manual workers to vote Labour".

Where associations are demonstrated on the basis of distributions in sample populations, it is necessary to check that these associations have not arisen because of some accident of sampling, that is to say that they are likely to occur in the universe from which the sample was drawn as well as in the sample. Tests of significance can be applied which, based on statistical theory, indicate the probability that the association shown in the sample is a chance occurrence. The detail of such tests will not be gone into here. They are dealt with in any textbook on statistics. Such tests are important and necessary, but one of the dangers inherent in their use is that they may give an impression of spurious accuracy. In addition, as Moser says, "In drawing conclusions from a significance test, the researcher runs two risks: (1) of rejecting the hypothesis when in fact it is true; and (2) of accepting the hypothesis when in fact it is false".[4] In the example given above the differences are so large that a test would certainly show them to be significant, and more important here, show the *level* of significance. An interesting example of a significance test applied to an allied problem can be found in Blalock.[5]

To show results to large numbers of decimal places may also give an impression of spurious accuracy. In fact there is a good case for rounding to the nearest integer and thinking in terms of "about 2%" because errors due to sampling, inaccurate response, and non-response may be substantial depending on the size of the sample, the structure of the questionnaire, and so on. Fine differences can become important if a whole series of small trends all point in the same direction. This would make one think that there is "something in it". In other circumstances one must beware of placing much confidence on small differences because of the large number of sources of impurity in social science data of most kinds.

It is most unlikely in analyses of this kind that any statements stronger than ones which begin "there is a tendency for . . ." will be able to be made about any of the relationships that are demonstrated. This is because although there are undoubtedly patterns in social behaviour, each individual is idiosyncratic and occupies, as Simmel showed many years ago,[6] a position in his society which is not *exactly* replicated by anybody else. What happens when people are taken in the mass is that patterns can be traced, but there are always a number of individuals who fall outside the pattern, because for them other tendencies are more strong, for them the combination of factors has worked out differently. Where, however, there is an apparent disparity in the pattern of behaviour, a research worker is encouraged to look below the surface of the first observations. The fact that there is *not* a very high correlation between being working class and voting Labour, while the middle class may be said in general to vote Conservative, suggests social rather idiosyncratic behaviour and leads the social researcher on to examine further. Much work has been done on this phenomenon, sometimes referred to as the "problem of the working class Tory".[7] One attempt to push the analysis further was made in a study of Newcastle-under-Lyme. Bealey *et al.* in this work[8] began by

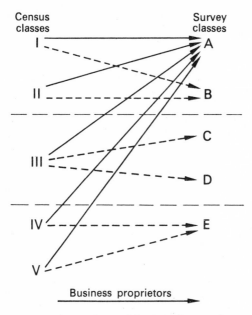

FIG. 2. Bealey *et al's.* modification of census classes.

classifying occupations on the basis of a modified census classification (p. 148) to ensure that all employers of labour were placed in one class, it being supposed that this characteristic might effect their voting behaviour. Their diagram, reproduced here as Fig. 2, shows the way in which the census classes were modified by these authors. The census classes referred to here are those defined and described in the publication *Classification of Occupations*.[9] The object of reorganizing them was to demonstrate statistically significant associations between class and voting. The disadvantages of doing this, as the authors point out, "is the difficulty of comparing it with findings in other places". Bealey *et al.* found that business proprietors and people in professional and managerial occupations were "overwhelmingly Conservative" (p. 169); that "taken together, the three non-manual sections of the population voted Conservative at the rate of just over 4 to 1", while manual workers divided in the ratio of 2 : 1 in favour of the Labour Party. The distribution is shown in Table 3. When thinking in terms of absolute numbers of votes it is, of course, important to remember that manual workers form a large majority of the total population.

Bealey examined other influences on voting such as age, sex, religion, school-leaving age, and owner-occupation, paying particular attention to the relation between self-assigned class and voting. Self-assigned class is the class which people say they belong to as opposed to the census category they would be put in on the basis of their (or, in the case of married women, their husbands') occupation. As Table 4 shows, there is some tendency for persons in manual occupations who call themselves "middle class" or "lower middle class" to vote Conservative. However, as Bealey *et al.* point out, on its own the fact that an association is shown between these two phenomena is not an "explanation" of either of them. The association is interesting, nevertheless, and was demonstrated by sorting first, manual and non-manual groups by voting behaviour, and then re-sorting the manual and non-manual groups into subgroups based upon self-assigned class. It is this method of analysis which this example is here used to demonstrate. There are limits to which this process can be pushed because the number of cases in each cell of the table become too small.[10] For these reasons, or others, sometimes all an analyst can do, having taken his data as far as he can, is to record whatever he may know about a category which behave "untypically" and say "Here we have the subject for a further piece of research."

It might be, however, that the researcher had tested his hypothesis on groups which he had also observed in the field and about

TABLE 3. PERCENTAGE CLASS AND 1959 GENERAL ELECTION VOTE (AFTER BEALEY)

Party	Percentage business proprietors	Percentage professional and managerial	Percentage clerical workers	Percentage skilled manual	Percentage less skilled manual	Total
Conservative	A 87	B 85	C 72	D 43	E 22	47
Labour	13	15	28	57	78	53
Percentage of sample in each group	9·0	10·5	8·4	37·3	32·1	97·3[a]

[a] The table excludes unemployed women without husbands (X), who were 2·7% of the sample. (From Table 2, p. 168, Bealey, Blondel, and McCann[8])

TABLE 4. PERCENTAGE CLASS, SELF-ASSIGNED CLASS, AND 1959
GENERAL ELECTION VOTE (AFTER BEALEY)

Party	Non-manual (A, B, and C)		Manual (D and E)	
	Self-assessment: "working class"	Other	Self-assessment: "working class"	Other
Conservative	28	72	54	46
Labour	81	19	76	24

From Table 9, p. 176, Bealey, Blondel, and McCann.[8]

which he had kept systematic records as well as undertaking a sample survey. In that case, having reached the limits of what he could infer from the statistics before him, he could return to these other records, seek out the cases who deviated and in this way get a clue to their behaviour.

At the start of this chapter it was supposed that the sorting into piles of cases all bearing the same characteristic (in this case party, income, and occupation) was done by hand, the questionnaires physically being placed in the relevant piles. For small surveys containing a lot of data, where there are numbers perhaps less than fifty, this is probably the best way of proceeding even nowadays. Where numbers are larger than this there is a good case for using some mechanical means of sorting. Also, in either case, if the schedules are likely to be worn out by much handling there is a case for transcribing the record so that there is a duplicate copy available. If a mechanical method is used this transcription will be by a code number representing a particular response and punched into a card. The simplest form of manually operated mechanical sorting is provided by Cope-Chat cards and a Paramount sorter. This is often known as the *knitting-needle technique*. The principle is simple. A card is used which has numbered holes punched all round the edge as illustrated in Fig. 3. For each of the responses possible a code number is given. One card is taken to represent one questionnaire. In our examples the following coding system might have been developed.

TABLE 5.

AN ILLUSTRATION OF CODING FOR COPE-CHAT

Code number 1 ⎫
             2 ⎪
             3 ⎬ Retained for identification of the case
             4 ⎭
             5   Party A
             6   Party B
             7   Party C
             8   Don't vote
             9   Don't know, refused and non-contact
            10   Wealthy (i.e. incomes £1500 and over)
            11   Poor (i.e. incomes less than £1500)
            12   Income unknown or no income
            13   Non-manual (defined by a list of occupations such as the
                  Standard Occupational Classification of the Registrar-
                  General).
            14   Manual (as above)
            15   Occupation unknown or no occupation

Here the first four codes are reserved for identification, the next five relate to party voting. Codes 5, 6, and 7, showing the party allegiance, and 8 and 9, those who gave no allegiance. In this case an attempt is made to separate those who don't vote (which is a positive action of non-co-operation with the political system) from those who refused to co-operate with the survey, were not found or who said they didn't know how they would vote. Codes 10 and 11 separate the two income groups (in practice one would almost certainly want more than this) and code 12 covers those who cannot be classified by income. Again, for some purposes one might want to divide those whose income is unknown (but they are known to have one) from those who have no income. It depends on the purpose of the survey. This would also apply to code 15, the residual occupation category.

In analysis it is necessary to take account of the size of the residual category even if one does not propose to use it. In the first sort, described at the beginning of this chapter, careful account was taken of the residual category. It was pointed out that if the residual category is at all large (particularly if it is as large, or larger, than one of the main categories, or larger than the difference between them)

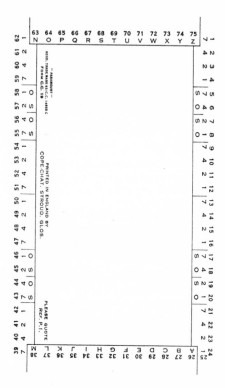

FIG. 3. Cope-Chat card.

special attention must be paid to it. In practice, one would always need to show somewhere the size of this group. The reason is of course that if an "unknown" or "unclassified" category is large it could materially alter the distribution one is concerned with, depending on how the unknowns, etc., are actually distributed.

Having determined the codes and allocated a card to each case, the relevant holes in the side of the Cope-Chat or similar card are then opened by a punch. Thus a Party A voter has his 5 hole opened and a Party B voter his 6 hole and so on.

The cards are then sorted by sticking a "knitting needle" through the holes, each in turn. Thus if the spike is stuck through hole 5 all those who vote A will fall through, since this hole was opened in their case. They can then be counted. If it is desired to know further information about A voters this particular group can then be sub-sorted into wealth or occupation or age or any other relevant coded data. The principle is exactly the same as if one were counting by hand. The procedure is quicker and possibly more accurate especially if one has relatively little data about a lot of cases. In particular the fact that it is necessary to code all the responses makes certain that one has clearly defined the meaning of the categories used. In coding it should be possible to apply the definition consistently to all cases.

If there are a considerable number of cards, running, say, into hundreds, there is a good case for acquiring the use of a *sorting machine* if one is not immediately available. The data are once again transferred onto cards, probably of the type illustrated in Fig. 4. The principle is essentially the same. Each set of responses are given a code number. In this case, however, rather than the holes being all round the edge of the card they are punched in columns as can be seen. The normal procedure is to allocate a column to a question, or rather to a set of responses, again keeping a number of columns either at the start or at the end of the card for essential identification. The code we took before might, for example, now read something like the illustration in Table 6.

The most usual procedure, when the codes for all the data that is to be entered have been worked out, is to make them into a code book. This is built up simply by allocating a page to each column and here putting the code numbers and the relevant definitions. The sheets, one for each column, can be clipped together into a file to make the code book. Any redefinitions or omissions that are filled in during the course of coding can then be entered firmly into every copy of the code book. Code classifications should be clearly defined in this, for quite apart from changes in personnel it is surprising how a definition, which was clearly in the researcher's

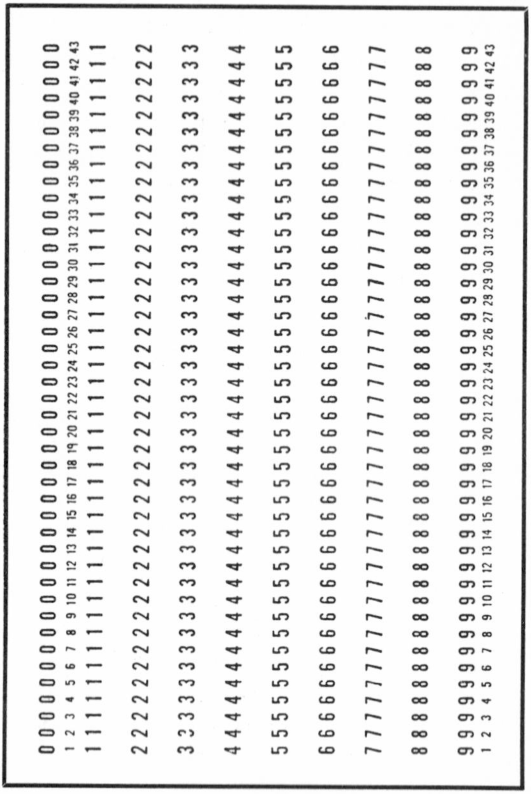

FIG. 4. I.B.M. card.

head when he first did the coding, has become blurred when he returns to it after a few months.

The cards, as can be seen from the illustration, have 80 columns and 10 places 0, 1, 2, 3, 4, . . . , 9 and a further two positions that can be used making a total of 12 alternative responses possible in

TABLE 6.

AN ILLUSTRATION OF CODING FOR MACHINE SORTING

		Code
Col. 1. Vote for:	Party A	1
	Party B	2
	Party C	3
	Don't vote	4
	Don't know, refused or non-contacts	5
Col. 2. Income:	Wealthy, i. e. incomes £1500 and over	1
	Poor, i. e. incomes of less than £1500	2
	Unknown or no income	3
Col. 3. Occupations:	Non-manual	1
	Manual	2
	Occupation unknown or no occupation	3

any one column. There are ways of making an increased number of responses possible per column, but these will not be discussed here. In any case they make sorting on the machine a good deal more complicated.[11]

When the cards are punched they are passed through the machine which will automatically sort them according to the instructions it is given, presenting them in a series of boxes. The sorters which are most useful for this kind of work have a counter on each box showing the number of cards that have been delivered in each, thus showing the distribution that has to be recorded on the analysis sheet.

Nowadays computers are becoming increasingly accessible and programs for simple sort routines and survey analysis are available. Data can be put on card or tape and analysed by computer. For this reason some may think it old-fashioned to explain in detail methods of hand and machine sorting. There are two reasons for doing this. Not all readers of this book, nor all survey analysers, will have a computer available to them. Modest surveys can still be done competently by hand or simple sorting machine. Second, there is a very good case for learning how to sort data by hand, before using a machine, so that the logic of each stage of the procedure is clear to the student. The machine will only do what it is instructed to and, if the research is to be meaningful, it is important that the worker should understand every stage of the analysis. It is well, therefore, to practise on a small study, manually analysed, before attempting anything so large that computer analysis is needed. The practice may be on the pilot stage of a larger study.

The value of a counter-sorter or computer is the speed with which it can work. Thus a machine can sort, in a few minutes, thousands of cards which would take many man-hours to sort by hand. Therefore, if more than, say, 1000 cases are to be dealt with, it is worth while putting the data on to punch cards and machine sorting. Where the analysis involves many repeated calculations, an electronic computer comes into its own. A computer made possible the study *British Towns* by Moser and Scott. This was based on a study of 157 towns in England and Wales and dealt with sixty variables relating to each. As they say: "The basic material for this analysis is the set of 1,635 coefficients [shown in Table 26] calculated in less than an hour by the high speed digital computer, "Mercury". If desk machines had been used, the job could have been done within a month only if forty skilled operators had been employed, and if it had been possible to organize them appropriately."[12] Moser and Scott do not say here how long the program took to write in the first place. Once a program is written, and proved to be satisfactory, the speed of computation is impressive. The difficulties of preparing and proving a program can be considerable and time must be allowed for this.

Since computers will only do what the operator tells them to do and can only work on the data fed in, a research worker who is swamped with data he does not know quite how to use will not be helped by a computer. A research worker who has a great deal of data and who is quite clear how he wants it to be used will find a computer invaluable. Since he knows exactly what he wants, he can get a program written and will save many man-hours of manual analysis. However, with data of a new kind one is often not quite clear how it should be analysed. In this case, even if there are several thousand cards involved, one may want "to think on the machine", that is, to use a sorter and to test out a series of working hypotheses on it. It is helpful if cards are used which can be fed both into a computer or into a sorting machine. In this case the large-scale analysis can be done on the computer, and checking and exploration on the sorter.

It is very likely that the complicated business of tabulation can be short-circuited on a computer as, for example, McKennell suggests by direct correlation analyses.[13] Undoubtedly these and other methods will become increasingly used as time goes on, since they mean that much more use can be made of survey data than has ever been possible in the past. The full range of uses of computers for the social sciences cannot be fully explored here. Readers are referred to specialist works on the subject.[14]

CONTENT ANALYSIS

This method is one which is particularly useful for the analysis of documentary evidence and has been referred to earlier in this connection. It is essentially a technique for reducing qualitative data to quantitative terms. It is well discussed by Goode and Hatt,[15] and its technique and uses for social-political research considered by Duverger.[16]

A recent example is the partial content analysis of a number of children's comics during three consecutive weeks. The object was to examine the presentation of nationality and of international killings or near killings in children's comics. Here the number of references under each of these two heads was counted for the period in question.[17] The careful content analyses undertaken by McClelland[18] have already been mentioned.

The method used in content analysis is to list the units to be measured and then to undertake a simple count of the items either of the whole works in question, or of a sample of them. One might be simply interested to know how much of certain publications were given over to pictures. In this case one would simply measure the column inches (in the case of a newspaper), or pages or part pages (in the case of a book) which were devoted to pictures in the total publication. The important factors are those which relate to any form of coding, namely that the categories into which the material is to be put are clear and unambiguous, that the same person doing the job later would recode the material in the same way and that someone else faced only with the defined categories and the codes would also code the matter in the same way.

Carol Owen has used content analysis to examine attitudes towards feminine roles and social mobility as expressed in women's weekly magazines.[19] Owen first isolated two social grades. She then, from examination of tables presented in the *National Readership Survey*,[20] isolated two groups of magazines: I, those read predominantly by the higher social grade, II, those read by the lower social grade. Fifty issues in each group published from June to October 1961 were taken as a basis for analysis. Indicators of feminine roles such as married, unmarried, widowed/divorced women, employed or unemployed, expressed desires for children, etc., were taken. Occupational, educational, income, and marriage references were used as indicators of social mobility. Each reference was counted once per character per story, counts being made of the frequencies with which the characters referred to the indicators. Each indicator was subdivided as to whether the reference was favourable or unfavourable and by the male or female origin of the reference. The results of this analysis of the contents were tested against the attributes of the total population. Thus it was found that fewer of the fictional women were employed, especially in group II magazines, than in the home population,[21] and in both groups, but especially in group II, far more fictional women than real women were single. The results of her content analysis led Owen to conclude that there were certain clear differences in the image of an acceptable woman put before group I compared with that put before group II readers. The former, for example, are more likely to work before marriage in a professional occupation than the latter, and are more likely to look forward to motherhood. The group II fictions departed much more widely from reality than the group I, and from this Owen concludes that the function of popular fiction in the lower group is escape and tension release, while in the higher group it is reinforcement of reality values.

OTHER TYPES OF ANALYSIS

The analysis of social groups, and of interaction processes, may not proceed by the counting of individuals so much as by the tracing of interconnections. Thus the analysis of the overlapping leadership of members of voluntary associations in Banbury described on pp. 103–5 was one such. The analysis of kinship systems where one is concerned to trace particular kinds of relationships between kin is another.[22] The plotting and analysis of networks of friends and other social contacts is a third.[23]

Reference has already been made to the experimental work of Bales reported in *Interaction Process Analysis*.[24] In this work observations of small groups in a laboratory setting were recorded in twelve categories. These categories were condensed from an originally much longer list which Bales had derived from theoretical premises (Fig. 5). The material was therefore collected in a form ready for analysis. The recordings can be analysed in a number of ways showing the interaction profile of an individual or a group. The individual profile shows the frequency of interaction of a group member, the type of his interaction, the role he played in the group. A group profile reveals the property of a group and its methods of approaching a problem-solving exercise and its degree of success. By analysing the output and intake of individual group members their differential use of channels of communication can be shown, a method of analysis similar to that of Bavelas referred to earlier. Group interaction may also be analysed over time, showing how this varies during different phases of the time span of any one session.

Helene Borke[25] has recently used a classification system to analyse family interaction with the ultimate aim of showing the normal transmission of behaviour patterns in the family over successive generations. In this case family interaction was observed and tape recorded in two situations, (i) a formal dinner, and (ii) solving four structured family tasks. The tapes were transcribed and then classified by judges while reading the transcript and at the same time listening to the tape. The classification was based on

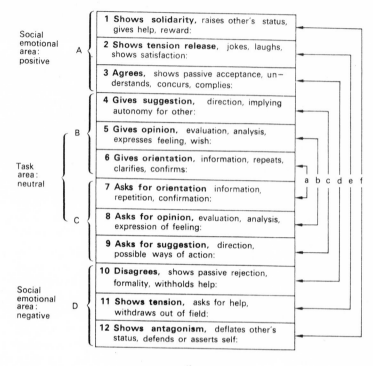

Key:
a Problems of communication
b Problems of evaluation
c Problems of control
d Problems of decision
e Problems of tension reduction
f Problems of reintegration

A Positive reactions
B Attempted answers
C Questions
D Negative reactions

FIG. 5. Bales's system of categories.

verb–adverb combinations to describe individual communication units grouped under Horney's broader classification.[26] This yielded the following categories of intent.

I. Goes towards other

1. Contributes
   (a) offers information
   (b) seeks information
   (c) entertains
   (d) miscellaneous

2. Supports
   (a) actively promotes
   (b) shows concern

3. Petitions
   (a) seeks support
   (b) seeks attention
   (c) seeks direct gratification

4. Directs
   (a) organizes
   (b) behaves strategically
   (c) instructs

5. Accepts from others
   (a) accepts support
   (b) accepts other's point of view

II. Goes against other

1. Resists
   (a) ignores
   (b) opposes actively

2. Attacks
   (a) behaves provocatively
   (b) attacks directly

III. Goes away from other

1. Retreats
   (a) evades
   (b) withdraws

The analysis of the five 3-minute samples from each tape $(1-1\frac{1}{2}$ hours long) proceeds in two stages. The first considers the structure of the interaction and the second the meaning. In the first stage each communication is identified and numbered, from whom and to whom it passed and whether it was an action or response or both. In the second stage the direction of the communication (towards, against or away from) and the intent of the communicator are determined. The analysis may then be presented in two forms: "molecular analysis", in which each person's action in relation to others is analysed, again yielding profiles; and process analysis, a more holistic approach focusing on the ongoing communication.

The findings are related to expectations based on roles likely to be played by members according to their age, sex, and family position.

Erving Goffman uses a particular type of non-numerate analysis of social relationships. He tends to be concerned with individuals as members of groups or categories in social situations. Thus in his examination of "total institutions" (prisons, mental hospitals, monasteries, and other "encompassing" establishments) he separates the life of the inmates from that of the staff.[27] He then separates various phases of the life of the inmate showing the character and content of each. In *The Presentation of the Self in Everyday Life*[28] Goffman developed the idea of the theatrical performance as a method of analysis, or model as he calls it. There he uses it to analyse "the way in which the individual in ordinary work situations presents himself and his activity to others".[29] In *Asylums*, his work about total institutions, Goffman draws upon empirical data, much of it non-numerate, such as diaries and accounts of persons who have lived in such establishments. Similarly, in *The Presentation*, as he says, "The illustrative materials used in this study are of mixed status: some are taken from respectable researches where qualified generalizations are given concerning reliably recorded regularities; some are taken from informal memoirs written by colourful people; many fall in between"; in addition he uses a field study of his own.[30]

Thus Goffman shows how the model of the drama can be used for analytical purposes. Many other models can and have been taken. In general they may be said to be aids for taking apart and showing the working connections between (i.e. analyzing) social relations. The aid or model is used by analogy from the parts of the known model. One of the oldest of such models is, of course, the organism: the idea that society is like an organism, made up of different parts each of which has a function to perform which contributes to the life of the whole. There are certain grave disadvantages to this as to almost any other model which is used for social analysis. Machines have also been used as models and are also found to be revealing in some respects and wanting in others. The whole subject, verging closely upon sociological theory as it does, is too complicated to consider in detail here.[31] It is important to grasp, however, that there can be systematic analysis which is not necessarily numerate analysis. Indeed, just as one piece of research may involve several methods of data collection so is it likely to involve several methods of analysis. Some of these will be numerate and some will not. The analysis of the social system of Banbury is an example.

In addition it is clear that whatever numerate analysis is attempted, and however precisely within its own limits it is conducted, it will be limited by the frame within which it was conceived, i.e. by the model of society which implicitly or explicitly was the basis of the research design.

REFERENCES

1. See, for example, E. L. SCHUSKY, *Manual for Kinship Analysis*, Holt, Rinehart & Winston, 1965; J. BEATTIE, *Understanding an African Kingdom: Bunyoro*, Holt, Rinehart & Winston, 1965.

2. See especially R. S. MILNE and H. C. MACKENZIE, *Marginal Seat*, Hansard Society, 1958; and M. BENNEY, *et al.*, *How People Vote*, Routledge and Kegan Paul, 1956.

3. STACEY, M., *Tradition and Change: A Study of Banbury*, O.U.P., 1960, pp. 41, 42.

4. MOSER, C. A., *Survey Methods in Social Investigation*, Heinemann, London, 1958, pp. 69, 70, 293, 294.

5. BLALOCK, H. M., *Social Statistics*, McGraw-Hill, 1960, p. 219.

6. SIMMEL, G., *Die Kreuzing sozialer Kreise* (literally "The Intersection of Social Circles"), trans. by R. Bendix as "The web of group affiliations", in G. SIMMEL, *Conflict and the Web of Group Affiliations*, trans. by K. H. Wolff and R. Bendix.

7. See, for example, D. LOCKWOOD, The "new working class", *European J. Sociol.*, **1** (2) 1960; J. H. GOLDTHORPE, D. LOCKWOOD, F. BECHHOFER, and J. PLATT, The affluent worker and the thesis of embourgeoisement: some preliminary research findings, *Sociology* **1** (1) (Jan. 1967); E. A. NORDLINGER, *Working Class Tory*, MacGibbon & Kee, 1967.

8. BEALEY, F., BLONDEL, J., and McCANN, W. P., *Constituency Politics: A Study of Newcastle-under-Lyme*, Faber & Faber, 1965.

9. *Classification of Occupations*, H.M.S.O., 1950, was the volume Bealey *et al.* used. There is now a 1966 edition available.

10. For a more detailed discussion of multi-variate analysis see P. F. LAZARSFELD, and M. ROSENBERG, *The Language of Social Research*, Free Press, New York, 1955, Section II.

11. For a further discussion of this see Moser, *op. cit.*, pp. 269 *et seq.* and the bibliography, p. 287.

12. MOSER, C. A. and SCOTT, W., *British Towns: A Statistical Summary of their Social and Economic Differences*, Oliver & Boyd, 1961, p. vii.

13. MCKENNELL, A. C., Correlational analysis of social survey data, *Sociol. Rev.* **13**, 1965.

14. For example, B. F. GREEN, *Digital Computers in Research: An Introduction for Behavioural and Social Scientists*, McGraw-Hill, 1963; H. BORKO, (Ed.), *Computer Applications in the Behavioural Sciences*, Prentice-Hall, 1962; and D. H. HYMES (Ed.), *The Use of Computers in Anthropology*, London, Mouton, 1965.

15. GOODE, W. J., and HATT, P. K., *Methods in Social Research*, McGraw-Hill, 1952, chap. 19.

16. DUVERGER, M., *Introduction to the Social Sciences*, Allen & Unwin, London, 1964, pp. 105 *et seq.*

17. JOHNSON, N., What do Children learn from War Comics?, *New Society* **197,** 1966.

18. MCCLELLAND, D. C., *The Achieving Society*, Van Nostrand, 1961.

19. OWEN, C., Feminine roles and social mobility in women's weekly magazines, *Sociol. Rev.* **10** (3), 283 *et seq.* (Nov. 1962).

20. THE INSTITUTE OF PRACTITIONERS IN ADVERTIZING, *National Readership Survey, The Supplementary Tables Sept. 1959–June 1960*, London, 1960.

21. *1951 Census, One Per Cent Sample Tables*, Pt. 1, H.M.S.O., London, 1952. *Registrar-General's Statistical Review*, 1959. *England and Wales Population Tables*, H.M.S.O., London, 1961.

22. For example, SCHUSKY, *op. cit.;* and M. G. SMITH and G. L. KRUIJER, *A Sociological Manual for Extension Workers in the Caribbean*. Caribbean Affairs Series, U.C. of the W. Indies, 1957.

23. For example, J. A. BARNES, Class and committees in a Norwegian island parish, *Human Relations* **7,** 39–58 (1954); J. A. BARNES, Genealogies, in A. L. EPSTEIN (Ed.) *The Craft of Social Anthropology*, Tavistock, 1967. E. BOTT, *Family and Social Network*, Tavistock, 1957; A. L. EPSTEIN, The network and urban social organization, *Rhodes–Livingstone Inst. J.* **29,** 29–62 (1961); and A. C. MAYER, The significance of quasi-groups in the study of complex societies, in M. BANTON (Ed.), *The Social Anthropology of Complex Societies*, p. 97.

24. BALES, R. F., *Interaction Process Analysis*, Addison-Wesley, 1950.

25. BORKE, H., The communication of intent: a systematic approach to the observation of family interaction; *Human Relations*, 1967, p. 13.

26. HORNEY, K., *Our Inner Conflicts*, Norton, New York, 1945.

27. GOFFMAN, E., *Asylums: Essays on the social situation of mental patients and*

other inmates, Anchor, New York, 1961.

28. GOFFMAN, E., *The Presentation of the Self in Everyday Life,* Anchor, New York, 1959.

29. *Ibid.,* p. xi.

30. *Ibid.,* pp. xi, xii.

31. See P. S. COHEN, Models, *Brit. J. Sociol.* **17** (1966), and M. BANTON (Ed.), *The Relevance of Models for Social Anthropology,* Tavistock, London, 1965.

CHAPTER 9

Presenting the Findings

THIS chapter draws not only on the writer's own experience in compiling research reports, but on Selltiz et al.[1] whose exposition of how to present a research report is both lucid and helpful.

The first things that must be decided in preparing the report are for whom it is to be written, whether it is to be published, and if so in what form. The audience will affect the manner and order of presentation. The old adage of the teacher "proceed from the known to the unknown" is a good guide in the presentation of any new findings. It immediately shows the way in which readership must be considered. What do the readers know? What information can be assumed? What is their starting point? To communicate successfully one must therefore know something about the people whom one is addressing, understand what is their interest in the research, and how much knowledge they have of the subject.

Thus a research report addressed to fellow academics can assume a completely different kind of knowledge from a research report addressed to the lay steering committee of an applied research project. In the first case one can assume detailed knowledge of other findings and reference to these will suffice. This assumption would be inappropriate in the second case, but here one can assume a detailed knowledge of certain practical aspects of the subject.

In some research it may be necessary to make more than one report. It is essential to communicate research results, as Selltiz et al. point out, and sometimes communication to more than one audience may be called for. This may be particularly true in applied research, where the brief only requires that there should be recommendation for action, but the research process may well have turned up findings which should be communicated to the profession through academic journals. These findings may be of no particular interest, or indeed relevance, to the applied problem and therefore should not be stressed in that report.

Although the style and emphasis of the presentation will vary according to the audience, the general principles which govern the presentation of any report remain the same. The general principles are that the researcher should say what he set out to do (object), how he did it (method), what came out of it, both negative and positive (results), and what he finally concluded from this.

Thus the report should start with the *object* of the research and include the theoretical, specific, and, where relevant, practical aims. It should then describe the research procedure as it actually took place, that is the *methods*. In many pieces of research more than one method will have been used, and, to achieve the overall aims, the research will have probably been broken down into subsidiary objectives. This sometimes leads to problems at the report stage. If the report is organized round the methods used and their individual results, it may lack coherence. Clearly it is better organized round the objects of the research. Thus if one object has been to find out the relationship between political and religious adherence in a particular town, two methods might have been used: one, to ask a sample of the population what their adherences were, and two, to find out the connections between religious and political leaders. Here the two methods can be described, the individual results from each reported separately and then the combined conclusion from the two methods discussed. If this object (the relation between religious and political adherence) was a sub-object of a larger exercise, as it has been in many community studies, for example, then the problem is more complicated. The best way then would seem to be to put the results together under the heading of the relevant sub-object as it logically follows in the argument of the research design, referring to the results as following from a particular method which is described elsewhere, perhaps in an appendix.

The order in which the "object, method, results, conclusion" are reported, need not be invariable as long as reference is made to them consistently and each is to be easily found at some place in the report. It should be clear throughout what is the evidence for every statement and what order of confidence can be played in it.

From this discussion it can be seen that there are a number of ways, within the overall principles, in which a report can be presented. Before the researcher starts writing his report he should have drawn up an outline of the way in which he proposes to do it. This would consist of headings and sub-headings and an indication of the way, under each of these, he proposes to gather together his data. At this stage decisions, such as whether detailed descriptions of the method are to be put in an appendix or in the text, and so on, may be made. The outline should be carefully examined for relevance and for logic. Within each section the relevance of the evidence to the object must be tested. The conclusions must only be those which can be substantiated from the evidence presented.

It may seem hard to think through the whole report in skeleton form at the beginning, but it is well worth while and makes the final writing process much quicker. The reorganizing of a few outline pages is after all a much smaller job than the reorganising of large and numerous sheets of writing. Sections of the research may already have been written up in an order other than that in which it is to go into the final report. Any wise researcher writes up sections as he goes along. An exploratory piece of research is harder to organize at this stage, as at others, than is one where fairly clear hypotheses are being tested. If the exploration has revealed anything at all it should be possible to organize the evidence around the propositions to which the exploration has led.

The report should start, as has been said, with a statement of the objects of the research. A difficulty can arise when the original objectives are changed. The aims as stated at the outset may have proved impossible of achievement, or proved to have been based upon a false assumption. In this case the research direction may have changed. If this occurs it should be stated quite clearly why and how it was decided to make this change and how the objectives were modified. Thus, in the Banbury study[2] the original aim had been to analyse the relations between Banburians and immigrants to the town. As the research proceeded it was found that the observed symptoms, which had led to this objective being set up, were symptoms not of a straightforward Banburian-immigrant division, but to a division between a traditional social system on the one hand and non-traditional social groups on the other. The objective changed, therefore, to one of examining this traditional–non-traditional division. To have stuck rigidly to the first intention would have been to produce partial correlations of behaviour with place of origin. The analysis would have missed altogether an interesting aspect of the structure and culture of the town, its implications for the social class system, and for processes of social change.

The results of the first would have been unlikely to have had interesting implications for sociological theory; the findings of the modified objects do have such implications. In presenting a report, however, it is most important to show any such changes in objects or proposed methods that have occurred, including the explanations for the changes.

Having thus set out the objects and the actual methods used the next thing is to display the findings. The findings of social research can be displayed in words, in tables, in diagrams, in maps, and sometimes even in three-dimensional models. Which form of presentation is used, or in what combinations they are used, depends on the nature of the research and also a good deal on the audience, not all of whom may be very great readers.

Inevitably a large proportion of any report will be in words and these can be easily misinterpreted. In the social sciences words used in a technical sense also have lay uses. Technical language cannot be avoided: words must have a clearly defined and limited meaning commonly accepted in the profession. This means that non-specialists must learn the definitions and should not expect to find an article in a professional journal easy to understand on first reading. It also means that reports for lay consumption must be adequately translated. At the present moment there is not always complete consensus about the technical use of words, so that where they are being used in a special sense it is necessary to make the definition clear. But the use of properly defined words in a technical sense does not necessarily mean that they should be long and complicated, or that sentences should be unnecessarily cumbersome and involved. Technical language should make the subject quicker and easier for the expert to understand or make something new intelligible. If it does neither of these things, it is inappropriate.

Whether using technical terms or not clarity of style is essential. As Selltiz *et al.* put it: "little can be said about [style], except to stress the value of simplicity and grammatical structure." We may not have agreement on our own technical vocabulary, but there is consensus about grammatical rules and, as Selltiz *et al.* point out, it aids successful communication if these are followed. They wisely advise against pretentiousness, saying that "there is no good reason for consistently using four-syllable words instead of one-syllable words with essentially the same meaning. Similarly, two or three relatively simple sentences may convey an idea more clearly than one complicated sentence with a number of entangled clauses."[3] This is a case for the dictum "If you can't say it simply, don't say it". Long and entangled sentences and many multi-syllable words sometimes turn out to be a cover for a good deal of confusion.

Most social research will have involved some statistical material. There is a minimum number of items of information which should always be presented about the subjects of social research.* Usually one needs to know the total number, age, sex, marital status, and occupation of the population that is under discussion. These can all best be presented in tabular form, although a descriptive summary in the text is also helpful. Thus, one might say that "This was largely a population of young married junior executives" in the text. In addition, this may be more precisely recorded in a table (perhaps in an appendix). Other research results may depend almost exclusively on tabular presentation.

The importance of having the categories for tabulation clearly

*See Appendix 1 for a list of suggested minimum facts any survey should report.

defined was indicated in Chapter 7. The way a table itself is presented is important. It should always have a serial number and a descriptive title to identify it. It should indicate its source and to what denominations the figures relate: number in sample; per cent; mean, etc. Columns down and rows across should all be clearly labelled and this should be done in each table. A convention should be consistently followed throughout about the use of empty cells, dashes, 0, etc., to avoid confusion between those where zero value is indicated and those where there is no information.

Data which are presented graphically or in maps should also always be clearly numbered and labelled, the key to symbols being given in each case, the values and subjects of ordinates being clearly expressed. Maps and diagrams should never try to say too much at once. As two or three sentences are always better than one long and involved one, so are two or three maps better than one over-crowded one.

However it is presented, in words or otherwise, it is a rule of the scientific method that all the evidence should be presented: that which fits with the thesis and, as well, *that which is contrary to it*. In the course of the work it will have been the social scientist's business to look for the evidence that does not fit, to try, if he had a clear hypothesis, to disprove his case. It is now, at the report stage, his responsibility to report in full what he has discovered, even if it is contrary to his expectations. Negative findings are as important as positive ones, and may well turn out to be the basis upon which new discoveries are made.

It is also important to show how the findings relate to those of other studies, where they are in accord and where they differ. Frequently this calls for statistical comparisons which may present difficulties. The categories used by other researchers may not be the same. The intervals in a continuum (e.g. age groups) may differ, as may the definitions. If there are differences the researcher may have to make some adjustments. For this reason it is important that, at least for much commonly collected data, there should be agreement on categories and definitions. It is desirable that all research workers should collect data on the basis of common categories, even if they wish to use others of their own invention as well. In the absence of any other agreed classifications, data should be classified according to the categories used by the official government statisticians of the countries where the research is being done. This ensures that each piece of work may be compared with official data, and also that each piece of research may be compared with each other. In presenting the report the distribution for the research population should be shown against any relevant national distribution according to the same categories and definitions. They may also be shown according to any other categories which the research worker thinks are more appropriate to the immediate purpose of his report.

To show, in the report, the ways in which the research can be used for comparative purposes is as important as communicating the results of the research itself. Generally speaking the development of sociology must depend upon the application of the comparative method. In its turn this must depend on the secondary analysis of comparable data. Field research will only add its full measure to the sum total of the development of the subject if data can be presented in ways which make this easier.

Having written the report the time has come to read it through with check questions, similar to those suggested by Selltiz *et al*, in mind: Is this sentence clear? Is it grammatically correct? Does it say what I mean? Could it be expressed more simply? Does the evidence, including the tables, justify the conclusions drawn? Are the points logical? Are there any internal contradictions? Then, having corrected in response to these questions, the next step is to get someone else to read it. The final step will probably be to rewrite it, in whole or in part. Most writers have to rewrite a good deal at various stages. It is a necessary part of the process if you want to turn out a polished piece of work and no one new to the business of report writing should be discouraged by having to do so.

From this it can be seen that writing the report is by no means a small part of the whole research process. As with analysis, all too often inadequate time is allowed for it. Quite how long it takes, in relation to data collection and analysis, depends a good deal on the extent to which interim reports have been written and on the kind of research. Research in which the results of investigations by different methods in slightly different areas have to be synthesized will naturally take longer than a piece which depends on one method in one area only. Research, the importance and relevance of which can only be demonstrated by comparison with other studies, or with official statistics, also requires more time at the write-up stage. But, as Selltiz *et al.* says, "if sufficient time has been allowed for preparation of the report (which is seldom true), the investigator may even find himself enjoying the opportunity it presents to fit pieces together into a larger whole, to consider the implications of his findings, to mull over the gaps or new questions raised and to think about what kind of future research might provide the answers".[4]

REFERENCES

1. SELLTIZ, C., JAHODA, M., DEUTSCH, M., and COOK, S. W., *Research Methods in Social Relations*, Henry Holt, 1959.
2. STACEY, M., *Tradition and Change: A Study of Banbury*, O.U.P., 1960.
3. SELLTIZ *et al.*, *op cit.*, p. 452.
4. *Ibid.*, p. 442.

Minimum Items to include in a Social Research Report*

1. By whom, for whom, and with what financial backing the research was undertaken.
2. The objects of the research.
3. The time at which the field work was undertaken and its duration.
4. The universe which was the subject of the research, including basic demographic details.
5. The details of any samples taken which should include: the size of the sample; the sample fraction; the method of sampling; the number of completed interviews related to the number of planned interviews.
6. Descriptions of the methods of data collection: whether from documents, observation, or interview and the type of each used.
7. Details of the staff employed and their supervision.
8. A copy of any questionnaires, schedules, or interview guides used.
9. The facts found, including those contrary to the hypotheses.
10. Where data is presented in the form of percentages or other indices, tables should include the number of cases on which these were based.

*In drawing up this list I have been guided particularly by The Market Research Society, *Standards in Market Research*, Part IV, Standards in reporting on sample surveys, London, 1965, and by the National Institute for Social Work Training, *Research in the Personal Social Services: Proposals for a Code of Practice*, National Council of Social Service, London, 1965.

11. The relation of the evidence collected to comparable information collected in other studies.
12. As appropriate, the implications of the findings for previously stated theoretical propositions and/or for action.

Bibliography

This includes works on methodology as well as on elementary and more advanced techniques.

ABRAMS, M., *Social Surveys and Social Action*, Heinemann, 1951.

ANDERSON, N., *Our Industrial Urban Civilization*, Asia Publishing House, London, 1964.

ARENSBERG, C., KIMBALL, S. T., *Family and Community in Ireland*, Cambridge, 1948.

BALES, R. F., *Interaction Process Analysis*, Addison-Wesley, 1950.

BANTON, M. (Ed.), *The Social Anthropology of Complex Societies*, Tavistock, 1966.

BANTON, M. (Ed.), *The Relevance of Models for Social Anthropology*, Tavistock, London, 1965.

BARNES, J. A., Class and committees in a Norwegian island parish, *Human Relations* **7**, 39–58 (1954).

BARNES, J. A., The collection of genealogies, *J. Rhodes-Livingstone Inst.*, No. 5, pp. 48–55, Oxford.

BARNES, J. A., Some ethical problems in modern fieldwork, *Brit. J. Sociol.* **14**, 2 (1963).

BARNES, J. A., Genealogies, in A. L. EPSTEIN (Ed.), *The Craft of Social Anthropology*, Tavistock, 1967.

BAVELAS, A., Communication patterns in task-oriented Groups; in *Group Dynamics—Research and Theory*, Ed. D. Cartwright and A. Zander, Tavistock, 1960.

BEALEY, F., BLONDEL, J., and McCANN, W. P., *Constituency Politics: A Study of Newcastle-under-Lyme*, Faber & Faber, 1965.

BEATTIE, J., *Understanding an African Kingdom: Bunyoro*, Holt, Rinehart & Winston, New York, 1965.

BECKER, H. S., Problems of inference and proof in participant observation, *Am. Sociol. Rev.*, Dec. 1958.

BENDIX, R., Concepts and generalizations in comparative social studies, *Am. Sociol. Rev.* **28**, 536 (1963).

BENJAMIN, B., *Health and Vital Statistics*, Allen & Unwin, London, 1968.

BENJAMIN, B., *The Population Census*, SSRC, Heinemann, 1970.

BENNEY, M., *et. al.*, *How People Vote*, Routledge and Kegan Paul, London, 1956.

Beveridge Report, Cmd. 6404, H.M.S.O., London, 1942.

BLALOCK, H. M., *Social Statistics*, McGraw-Hill, New York, 1960.

BLAU, P. M., The research process in the study of the dynamics of bureaucracy, in P. Hammond (Ed.), *Sociologists at Work: Essays on the Craft of Social Research*, Basic Books, 1964.

BLUMER, H., An appraisal of Thomas and Znaniecki's "The Polish Peasant", *Social Science Res. Council Bulletin*. No. 44, 1939.

BOOTH, C., *Life and Labour of the People*, Vol. 1. Williams & Norgate, 1889.

BOOTH, C., *Labour and Life of the People*, Vol. 2, Macmillan, 1891

BOOTH, C., The inhabitants of the Tower Hamlets (School Board Division), their condition and occupations, *J. Roy. Stats. Soc.* 1887, pp. 326–91.

BORKE, H. The communication of intent: a systematic approach to the study of family interaction, *Human Relations*, 1967.

BORKO, H. (Ed.), *Computer Applications in the Behavioural Sciences*, Prentice-Hall, 1962.

BOSSARD, J. H. S. and BOLL, E. S., *The Large Family System*, Univ. of Pennsylvania Press, 1956.

BOTT, E., *Family and Social Network*, Tavistock, 1957.

BRUYN, S. T., *The Human Perspective in Sociology: The Methodology of Participant observation*, Prentice-Hall, 1966.

CANNELL, C. F. and KAHN, R. L., *The Dynamics of Interviewing: Theory Techniques and Cases*, John Wiley, New York, 1957.

CARTWRIGHT, D. and ZANDER, A., *Group Dynamics—Research and Theory*, Tavistock, 1960.

CHRISTIE, R. and JAHODA, M. (Eds.), *Continuities in Social Research: Studies in Scope and Method of the Authoritarian Personality*, Free Press, 1954.

CICOUREL, A. V., *Method and Measurement in Sociology*, Free Press, 1964.

COHEN, P. S., Models, *Brit. J. Sociol.* **17,** 1966.

COLE, D. and UTTING, J. *The Economic Circumstances of Old People*, Occasional Papers on Social Administration, No. 4, Codicote, 1962.

CONNOLLY, T. G., and SLUCKIN, W., *An Introduction to Statistics for the Social Sciences*, Cleaver Hume, London, 1958.

COSER, L. (Ed.), *Georg Simmel*, Prentice-Hall, 1965.

DAVIS, A., GARDNER, B., and GARDNER, M. R., *Deep South: A Social Anthropological Study of Caste and Class*, Chicago, 1941.

DEPARTMENT OF EDUCATION AND SCIENCE, *Annual Reports, 1964, 1965, 1966* (previously published by Ministry of Education and before that, Board of Education). See also specialist pamphlets and circulars.

DEPARTMENT OF EDUCATION AND SCIENCE, *British Research and Development Reports*, National Lending Library for Science and Technology, Boston Spa, Yorks.

DEPARTMENT OF EDUCATION AND SCIENCE, *Report of the Committee on Social Studies*, Heyworth, Cmd. 2660, H.M.S.O.

DURKHEIM, E., *Suicide*, trans. J. A. Spaulding and G. Simpson (Ed.), (G. Simpson), Free Press, New York 1951.

DUVERGER, M., *Introduction to the Social Sciences*, Allen & Unwin, Minerva, London, 1964.

ELDER, G. H. JR., and BOWERMAN, C. E., Family structure and child rearing patterns: the effect of family size and sex composition, *Am. Sociol. Rev.* **28**, 891, 1963.

ELDER, G. H. JR, Structural variations in the child rearing relationship, *Sociometry* **25**, 252 (1962).

EPSTEIN, A. L. (Ed.), *The Craft of Social Anthropology*, Tavistock, 1967.

EPSTEIN, A. L., The network and urban social organization, *J. Rhodes-Livingstone Inst.* **29**, 29–62 (1961).

FESTINGER, L. and KATZ, D. (Eds.), *Research Methods in the Behavioural Sciences*, Staples Press, London, 1954.

FIRTH, R., *Malay Fishermen: their Peasant Economy*, Kegan and Paul, London, 1946. 2nd revised ed., Routledge and Kegan Paul, 1966.

FIRTH, Rosemary, *Housekeeping among the Malay Peasants*, 2nd edition, L.U. Athlone Press, 1966.

FORGE, A., The lonely anthropologist, *New Society*, 17 August 1967, pp. 221 *ff.*

FORTES, M. (Ed.), *Marriage in Tribal Societies*, C.U.P., 1962.

FRANKENBERG, R., Participant observation, *New Society*, **23**, 22 (1963).

FRANKENBERG, R., *Communities in Britain, Social Life in Town and Country*, Pelican, 1966.

FRANKENBERG, R., *Village on the Border*, Cohen & West, London, 1957.

GALLAHER, A. J., Plainville: the twice studied town, in A. J. Vidich, A. Bensman and M. R. Stein, *Reflections on Community Studies*, Wiley, New York, 1964.

GALTUNG, J., *Theory and Methods of Social Research*, Allen & Unwin, 1967.

GANS, H., *Urban Villagers*, Appendix on participant observation.

GENERAL REGISTER OFFICE, *Census*, decennial since 1801, except 1941; 10% *Sample Census*, 1966, H.M.S.O.

GENERAL REGISTER OFFICE, *Classification of Occupations, 1950*, H.M.S.O., 1951.

GENERAL REGISTER OFFICE, *Classification of Occupations, 1960*, H.M.S.O., 1961.

GENERAL REGISTER OFFICE, *Classification of Occupations, 1966*, H.M.S.O., 1966.

GENERAL REGISTER OFFICE, *Registrar-General's Annual Estimates of the Population of England and Wales and of Local Authority Areas*, H.M.S.O., London.

GENERAL REGISTER OFFICE, *Registrar-General's Statistical Review*, Appears annually in three parts: Part I, *Medical Tables*, Part II, *Population Tables*. Part III, *Commentary*.

GENERAL REGISTER OFFICE, *Studies on Medical and Population Subjects* (studies have appeared at intervals since the Second World War on various medical and population subjects), H.M.S.O., London.

GIBBS, J. P., *Urban Research Methods*, Van Nostrand, 1961.

GIBSON, Q., *The Logic of Social Enquiry*, Routledge and Kegan Paul, 1960.

GIDDENS, A., The suicide problem in French sociology, *Brit. J. Sociol.* **16**, 3 (1965).

GINSBERG, M., *On Justice in Society*, Heinemann, 1965.

GLASS, D. V. (Ed.), *Social Mobility*, Routledge and Kegan Paul, 1954.

GLUCKMAN, M. (Ed.), *Closed Systems and Open Minds: The Limits of Naïvety in Social Anthropology*, Oliver & Boyd, 1964.

GOFFMAN, E., *Asylums: Essays on the Social Situation of Mental Patients and Other Inmates*, Anchor, New York, 1961.

GOFFMAN, E., *The Presentation of the Self in Everyday Life*, Anchor, New York, 1959.

GOLDTHORPE, J. H., LOCKWOOD, D., BECHHOFER, F., and PLATT, J., The affluent worker and the thesis of embourgeoisement: some preliminary research findings, *Sociology* **1**, 1 (1967).

GOODE, W. J., and HATT, P. K., *Methods in Social Research*, McGraw-Hill, 1952.

GREEN, B. F., *Digital Computers in Research: An Introduction for Behavioural and Social Scientists*, McGraw-Hill, 1963.

GUETZKOW, H., Differentiation of roles in task-oriented groups, in D. Cartwright and A. Zander, *Group Dynamics—Research and Theory*, Tavistock, 1960.

HAMMOND, P. (Ed.), *Sociologists at Work: Essays on the Craft of Social Research*, Basic Books, 1964.

HAUSER, P. M. (Ed.), *Handbook for Social Research in Urban Areas*, Unesco, 1965.

HAUSER, P. M., et al., *Sample Survey Methods and Theory*, Wiley, 1953.

HEMPEL, C. G., *Aspects of Scientific Explanation and other Essays in the Philosophy of Science*, Collier–Macmillan, London, 1965.

HIGHET, J., *The Scottish Churches: A Review of their State 400 Years After the Reformation*, Skeffington, 1960.

HIGHET, J., *The Churches in Scotland Today: A Survey of their Principles, Strength, Work and Statements*, Jackson, 1950.

HOLE, V., *Children's Play on Housing Estates*, National Building Studies Research Paper, 39, H.M.S.O., London, 1966.

HORNEY, K., *Our Inner Conflicts*, Norton, New York, 1945.

HYMAN, H. H. et al., *Interviewing in Social Research*, Univ. of Chicago Press, 1955.

HYMAN, H. H. et al., *Survey Design and Analysis: Principles, Cases and Procedures*, Free Press, 1955.

HYMES, D. H. (Ed.), *The Use of Computers in Anthropology*, Mouton, London, 1965.

THE INSTITUTE OF PRACTITIONERS IN ADVERTIZING, *National Readership Survey, The Supplementary Tables, September 1959—June 1960*, London, 1960.

JOHNSON, N., What do Children Learn from War Comics? *New Society* **197**, 1966.

JUNKER, B. H., *Field Work: An Introduction to the Social Sciences*, Univ. of Chicago Press, 1960.

KAHAN, M., BUTLER D., and STOKES, D., On the analytical division of social class, *Brit. J. Sociol.* 1966.

KARSH, B., *Diary of a Strike*, Univ. of Illinois, 1958.

KIRK, H. D., *Shared Fate: A Theory of Adoption and Mental Health*, Free Press of Glencoe, 1964.

KISH, L., *Survey Sampling*, Wiley, 1965.

LAZARSFELD, P. F. and ROSENBERG, M., *The Language of Social Research*, Free Press, New York, 1955.

LEWIN, K., *Field Theory in Social Science*, Tavistock, 1963.

LEWIS, O., *Life in a Mexican Village: Tepoztlan Revisited*, Univ. of Illinois Press, 1951.

LIPPIT, R., and WHITE, R. K., An experimental study of leadership and group life, in G. E. Swanson, T. M. Newcomb, and E. L. Hartley, *Readings in Social Psychology*, Holt, New York, 1952.

LIPSET, S. M., and BENDIX, R., *Social Mobility in Industrial Society*, Heinemann, London, 1959.

LITTLEJOHN, J., *Westrigg: The Sociology of a Cheviot Parish*, Routledge and Kegan Paul, London, 1963.

LOCKWOOD, D., The "new working class", *European J. of Sociol.* **1,** 2 (1960).

LOWIE, R., Marriage, *Encyc. of Soc. Sciences*, 1933.

LUPTON, T., *On the Shop Floor: Two Studies of Workshop Organization and Output*, Pergamon, Oxford, 1963.

LYND, R. S., and LYND, H. M., *Middletown: A Study in American Culture*, Harcourt Brace, New York, 1929.

LYND, R. S., and LYND, H. M., *Middletown in Transition: A Study in Cultural Conflicts*, Harcourt Brace, New York, 1937.

LYNES, T., *National Assistance and National Prosperity*, Occasional Papers on Social Administration, No. 5, Codicote, 1962.

McCLELLAND, D. C., ATKINSON, J. W., CLARK, R. A., and LOWELL, E. L., *The Achievement Motive*, Appleton–Century–Crofts, 1953.

McCLELLAND, D. C., *The Achieving Society*, Van Nostrand, 1961.

MACIVER, R. M., *Society*, Farrar & Rinehart, 1937.

MACIVER, R. M., and PAGE, C. H., *Society: An Introductory Analysis*, MacMillan, 1950.

McKENNELL, A. C., Correlational analysis of social survey data, *Sociol Rev.* **13,** 1965.

MADGE, J., *The Tools of Social Science*, Longmans, 1965.

MADGE, J., *The Origins of Scientific Sociology*, Tavistock, 1963.

MALINOWSKI, B., Marriage, *Encyc. Brit.*, 1929.

MALINOWSKI, B., *Argonauts of the Western Pacific*, Routledge and Kegan Paul, 1964 (first published 1922).

MARKET RESEARCH SOCIETY, *Standards in Market Research*, revised January 1965.

MARTINDALE, D., *The Nature and Types of Sociological Theory*, Routledge and Kegan Paul, London, 1961.

150 BIBLIOGRAPHY

MAYER, A. C., The significance of quasi-groups in the study of complex societies, in M. Banton (Ed.), *The Social Anthropology of Complex Societies*, Tavistock, 1966.

MERTON, R. K., and KENDALL, P. L., *The Focused Interview*, Free Press, 1956.

MERTON, R. K., and LAZARSFELD, P. L. (Eds.), *Continuities in Social Research: Studies in the Scope and Method of "The American Soldier"*, Free Press, 1950.

MILLER, D. C., *Handbook of Research Design and Social Measurement*, McKay Social Science Series, 1964.

MILLS, C. W., *The Sociological Imagination*, O.U.P., 1959.

MILNE, R. S., and MACKENZIE, H. C., *Marginal Seat*, Hansard Society, 1958.

MINISTRY OF HEALTH, *Annual Reports*, London, H.M.S.O.

MINISTRY OF HEALTH, *Statistical Report Series*, H.M.S.O., London.

MINISTRY OF HEALTH, see also specialist publications, pamphlets, and circulars, etc., H.M.S.O., London.

MINISTRY OF EDUCATION, *See Department of Education and Science.*

MINISTRY OF HOUSING AND LOCAL GOVERNMENT, *Handbook of Statistics 1966*, H.M.S.O., 1967 (lists all major publications of the department during 1966).

MINISTRY OF LABOUR, *Family Expenditure Survey: Reports for 1957–9, 1960–1, 1962, 1963, 1964, 1965*, H.M.S.O., London.

MINISTRY OF LABOUR, *Ministry of Labour Gazette*, H.M.S.O., London.

MOORE, T., The London doll play technique, *J. Child Psychol. Psychiat.* **5**, 1964.

MOSER, C. A., and SCOTT, W., *British Towns: A Statistical Summary of their Social and Economic Differences*, Oliver & Boyd, 1961.

MOSER, C. A., *Survey Methods in Social Investigation*, Heinemann, London, 1958.

MUSSEN, P. H. (Ed.), *Handbook of Research Methods in Child Development*, Wiley, New York, 1960.

NAGEL, E., *The Structure of Science*, Harcourt Brace & World (1961).

NATIONAL INSTITUTE FOR SOCIAL WORK TRAINING, *Research in the Personal Social Services: Proposals for a Code of Practice*, Nat. Cl. of Soc. Service, London, 1965.

NORDLINGER, E. A., *Working Class Tory*, MacGibbon & Kee, 1967.

OGBURN, W. F., *On Culture and Social Change*, Phoenix, 1964.

OLMSTED, M. A., *The Small Group*, Random House, 1959.

OPPENHEIM, A. M., *Questionnaire Design and Attitude Measurement*, Heinemann, 1966.

OWEN, C., Feminine roles and social mobility in women's weekly magazines, *Sociol. Rev.* **10**, 3 (Nov. 1962).

PARTEN, M., *Surveys, Polls and Samples*, Harper, 1965.

PHILLIPS, A. (Ed.), *Survey of African Marriage and Family Life*, London, 1953.

POPPER, K., *The Logic of Scientific Discovery*, Hutchinson, 1959.

RADCLIFFE-BROWN, A. R. and FORDE, D. (Eds.), *African Systems of Kinship and Marriage*, O.U.P., 1950.

RICKMAN, H. P., *Understanding and the Human Studies*, Studies in Sociology, Heinemann, 1967.

RILEY, M. W. *et al.*, *Sociological Studies in Scale Analysis*, Rutgers Univ. Press, 1954.

ROETHLISBERGER, F. J., and DIXON, W. J., *Management and the Worker*, Harvard Univ. Press, Cambridge, Mass., 1939.

ROGERS, C. R., The non-directive method as a technique for social research, *Am. J. Sociol.* **50,** 279–83 (1945).

ROKKAN, S., Second conference on data archives in the social sciences, *Social Sciences Information*, **4** (1), 67 ff. (March 1965).

ROKKAN, S., and SCHEUCH, K., Conference on data archives in the social sciences, *Social Sciences Information*, 2 (4), 109 ff. (December 1963).

ROSE, A. M., *Theory and Method in the Social Sciences*, Univ. of Minnesota Press (1954).

ROSSER C., and HARRIS, C., *The Family and Social Change*, Routledge and Kegan Paul, London, 1965.

ROWNTREE, B. S., *The Human Needs of Labour*, Longmans (1937).

ROWNTREE, B. S., *Poverty: A Study of Town Life*, 1922.

ROWNTREE, B. S., *Poverty and Progress: A Second Social Survey of York*, Longmans, London, 1941.

SCHUSKY, E. L., *Manual for Kinship Analysis*, Holt, Rinehart & Winston, 1965.

SCHUTZ, A., Common-Sense and Scientific Interpretation of Human Action. *Phil. and Phenom. Research*, **14,** 1953.

SCHWARTZ, M. S. and SCHWARTZ, C. G., Problems in participant observation, *Am. J. Sociol.* **60,** 344 (1954–5).

SELLTIZ, C., JAHODA, M., DEUTSCH, M., COOK, S. W., *Research Methods in Social Relations*, Henry Holt, 1959.

SHAW, M. E., A comparison of two types of leadership in various communication nets, *J. Abnorm. Soc. Psychol.* **50,** 1955.

SIMEY, T. S. and SIMEY, M. B., *Charles Booth: Social Scientist*, O.U.P., 1960.

SIMMEL, G., *Conflict and the Web of Group Affiliations*, trans. K. H. Wolff and R. Bendix, Collier–Macmillan, London, 1955.

SMITH, M. G., KRUIJER, G. J., *A Sociological Manual for Extension Workers in the Caribbean*, Caribbean Affairs Series, U.C. of W. Indies, 1957.

SOCIAL SCIENCES INFORMATION, *Data Archives*, **4,** 3 (Sept. 1965); see also ROKKAN, S.

STACEY, M., *Tradition and Change: A Study of Banbury*, O.U.P., 1960.

STACEY, M. (Ed.) *Comparability in Social Research*, B.S.A./S.S.R.C., Heinemann, 1969.

STACEY, M. (Ed.), DEARDEN, R., PILL, R. and ROBINSON, D., *Hospitals, Children and their families*, Routledge and Kegan Paul, 1970 (forthcoming).

STOUFFER, S. A., *Measurement and Prediction*, Princeton, H. J., 1950.

SWANSON, G. E., NEWCOMB, T. N., and HARTLEY, E. L., *Readings in Social Psychology*, Holt, New York, 1952.

UNITED NATIONS BUREAU OF SOCIAL AFFAIRS, *Report on the World Social Situation*, 1958.

UNITED NATIONS EDUCATIONAL SCIENTIFIC AND CULTURAL ORGANIZATION, *Population and Culture Series*.

UNITED NATIONS STATISTICAL COMMISSION, *International Programme of Social Statistics*.

UNITED NATIONS STATISTICAL OFFICE, *Compendium of Social Statistics*.

UNITED NATIONS STATISTICAL OFFICE, *Demographic Year Book*.

VIDICH, A. J., Participant observation of the collection and interpretation of data, *Am. J. Sociol.* **60**, 357 (1954–5).

VIDICH, A. J., BENSMAN, J., and STEIN, M. R., *Reflections on Community Studies*, Wiley, New York, 1964.

WARNER, W. L. *et al.*, *Democracy in Jonesville*, Harper, New York, 1949.

WARNER, W. L., and LUNT, P. S., *The Social Life of a Modern Community*, Yankee City Series, No. 1, Yale Univ., New Haven, 1941.

WEBER, M., *The Methodology of the Social Sciences* (Ed. E. Shills and H. A. Finch), Free Press, 1949.

WEBER, M., *The Theory of Social and Economic Organization* (Ed. T. Parsons), Free Press Paperback, New York, 1964.

WEBER, M., *The Protestant Ethic and the Spirit of Capitalism*, trans. Talcott Parsons, Unwin University Books, 1965.

WHITAKER, I., The nature and value of functionalism in sociology, *Functionalism in the Social Sciences*, Monograph No. 5 of the American Academy of Political and Social Science, 1965.

WHYTE, W. F., *Street Corner Society*, Univ. Chicago Press, 1955.

WILLIAMS, W. M., *The Sociology of an English Village: Gosforth*, Routledge and Kegan Paul, London, 1956.

WILLER, D., *Scientific Sociology: Theory and Method*, Prentice-Hall, 1967.

WILSON, B., *Sects and Society: A Sociological Study of three Religious Groups in Britain*, Heinemann, 1961.

WRIGHT, H. G., Observational child study, in P. Mussen (Ed.), *Handbook of Research Methods in Child Development*, Wiley, New York, 1960.

YANG HSIN PAO, *Fact Finding with Rural People*, F. A. O. Development Paper, No. 52.

YOUNG, M. and WILLMOTT, P., *Family and Kinship in East London*, Routledge and Kegan Paul, London, 1957.

YOUNG, P. V. *Scientific Social Surveys and Research*, Prentice Hall, revised 1966.

ZELDITCH, M., Some methodological problems of field studies, *Am. J. Sociol.* **67**, 566–76 (1962).

ZETTERBERG, H. L., *On Theory and Verification in Sociology*, Bedminster, 1965.

ZNANIECKI, F., *The Method of Sociology*, Holt, Rinehart & Winston, New York, 1934.

Name and Title Index

153

Subject Index